Creating Abundant Wealth Workbook

LISA S. LARSEN, PsyD

Copyright © 2010 Lisa S. Larsen

All rights reserved.

ISBN: 0615447376
ISBN-13: 978-0615447377

DEDICATION

This book is dedicated to all the people who want to have abundant wealth in all areas of their lives. No matter where you start from, there is so much that you can do to create and appreciate the wealth that you want. You can do it! Don't let self-limiting beliefs, attitudes or behaviors stand in the way anymore.

CONTENTS

	Acknowledgments	vi
	Introduction	viii
1	Defining Wealth And Abundance	1
2	Examining Your Beliefs About Wealth & Abundance	14
3	Educating Yourself About Money and its Proper Management	35
4	Making Opportunities Happen	58
5	Sharing and Enjoying Your Wealth	75
6	Creating an Action Plan to Create Abundant Wealth in Your Life	80
	Pre-Workshop / Pre-Book Assessment	87
	Post-Workshop / Post-Book Survey	89
	About the Author	91

ACKNOWLEDGEMENTS

This book would not have been possible without the help of some very wonderful people. Glen Larsen, my awesome husband, was instrumental in supporting, encouraging, and shaping the formation of this book. Eileen Hammons, an incomparable communicator, gave encouragement and helpful editing. Drs. Patricia Emerson and Sharon Gerstenzang were supportive and encouraging and gave me some great ideas. Friends and family were positive and supportive, and I thank them too. Finally, my fellow Toastmasters at the Citywide Word Wizards club in Lancaster, CA gave me great feedback as I tried many of these ideas in speeches. It takes a village to raise a book!

Dear Reader,

At the end of this book are two surveys or assessments. These are intended for you to fill out before and after you read the book and/or take the extended seminar. If you would please take the time to complete them, it will help you clarify your mission in reading this book and doing the exercises. It can help me to understand what you want from the book and workshop, and how I can assist you in achieving your goals. If you are reading the book without taking the workshop, I would still love to hear your feedback so I can improve the book and better assist other readings in reaching their goals. Thank you in advance for your cooperation, time, and energy.

Sincerely, Lisa S. Larsen, PsyD

INTRODUCTION

What do you want in life that you don't already have? More money, better health, improved relationships with your loved ones, or a greater spiritual connection? I want you to have all that and more. I cannot guarantee that this book will provide all that for you, but I can promise you that I will do my best to help you explore those issues and develop a plan to achieve your goals.

First, let me ask you: what do you think stands in your way now? Some people feel unworthy, unmotivated, or just plain tired. Some people don't know what stands in their way. Others don't know where or how to get started. If you are curious about this and want to take a serious look at what is holding you back, please read on. I am eager to help you remove the obstacles that stand between you and all that you desire.

There are many good books available about making and investing money. When I read them I get good ideas. Yet the psychologist in me always wonders how these ideas would work for someone who doesn't have self confidence or other issues. I am aware of many obstacles that prevent people from achieving their goals, not just for wealth building but also other areas of their lives. I also think that one plan does not fit all people – what works for some people might not work for you. I have helped many people overcome the obstacles to achieving their goals in my private practice of psychotherapy. While this book and workshop will not cure any mental illness or substance abuse condition, it will provide a number of steps to help you achieve what you want by acknowledging and working through the belief patterns that you have about wealth and abundance.

We will also look at how you handle your existing resources. This includes spending, saving, investing, and sharing money, time and energy. All these behaviors can be done both responsibly and irresponsibly. Shining the light of awareness on these issues brings about positive change. This need not be a painful process. Instead, it can be a joyous journey down the river of abundant wealth. The level of your success depends on the attitude with which you approach the journey. You can move from reluctance and denial to responsibility and empowerment. However, you can't change what you don't know about.

Written exercises in this book will help you explore your relationship to wealth. They can be useful to you if you apply what you learn to your lives. If you are using this as part of a live workshop, it's best to do these exercises a week ahead of the workshop topic. That way you can give them your full attention, and you will get the most from this exploration. Like anything, you get out of this what you put into it.

We begin by defining abundance and wealth so that you know when you have it and when you don't. Abundant wealth in this book includes physical health, emotional, spiritual, and social wealth as well as financial abundance. This definition of wealth is more complete and healthier than what I read about in most self help books about wealth. Much of the information that I've read in the United States of America promotes a strictly financial view of wealth and abundance. The common sentiment seems to promote working until your hands bleed because there's someone else breathing down your neck, ready to overtake you if you let up. This seems to create unnecessary anxiety and stress. On the other side, doing nothing is also ineffective.

Some authors claim that visualizing our expectations causes what we want to magically materialize. Sounds nice, doesn't it? I don't believe it 100%, but it would be tempting to believe. You will learn to define wealth realistically and sensibly so that we can relate to wealth in a healthy, welcoming fashion. You will also learn to not obsess over wealth or have fantasy-based ideas about it. Obsessing about wealth is just as harmful as being overly casual. You will learn that you don't get rich just by saying or thinking the right things to yourself while sitting on the couch all day.

I think it is unhealthy to focus exclusively on the financial aspect of wealth. A healthy sense of abundance encompasses other important aspects of existence as well: physical and emotional health, spiritual well being, and social connectedness. People often put all their eggs in the financial basket and forsake other aspects of their lives all the time. They are often unhappy and don't appreciate the good in their lives; instead they grasp for what they don't yet have.

Following this section we start focusing more on financial wealth. However, that doesn't mean that it's the most important type of abundance. It makes other aspects of our lives more comfortable and possible. We will take a harmonious view of wealth and abundance into consideration when we create the action plan. That way you can enjoy abundant wealth in many aspects of your life.

We will spend a lot of time looking at your thoughts and feelings about wealth as it relates to yourself, your job, your boss (or your business if you're self-employed), and your customers. Changing your beliefs can remove any obstacles to abundance that could come from emotional baggage from the past. I think of abundance as a giant river. Some people's rivers flow more easily because they have removed the obstacles to wealth. They look at blockages as opportunities to learn, to better engineer the flow of their destinies. Other folks feel helpless or victimized when their river doesn't flow, or they take the blockages personally. Luckily, the river of abundance is generous and forgiving. By examining our beliefs, we can fine-tune the currents in the river, so that more abundance flows into your life.

Once you have examined your beliefs, it then becomes important to know what to do with the wealth that's flowing into your life. You will be educating yourself about money and its proper management. Here you will look at what you already have, and what to do so you get what you want. You will also examine how much you want, and why. You can then develop a framework for your existing wealth and learn how to build upon that through savings, investments, and wise financial choices. It is important to understand your financial affairs, investments and savings. Understanding your finances helps avoid making costly mistakes. Reading this section won't do you much good until you address underlying issues and beliefs that led to your current financial state. If you do not believe that you can have wealth, you will find a way to unconsciously sabotage your own efforts.

When you've discovered what's holding you back (limiting beliefs), where you are, and where you want to go, you will then focus on making opportunities happen to further your success. Sometimes people adopt just part of a new idea. Their expectations are to succeed without action or complete understanding of what they're doing. One friend of mine ,named Fred, heard about the Law of Attraction[1] and thought it was pretty neat. He just said daily affirmations about what he wanted and expected it to happen. However, Fred did not consider how he would follow through with actions. Needless to say, he did not get the desired results. Thus, Fred wound up feeling discouraged and angry.

You want to avoid falling into this trap. We will explore many ways to take action on our improved thoughts about money. Putting yourself in the path of opportunities is the way to accomplish this. We will look at different ways to let people know you're ready for business, so that you succeed. It's most effective to do this graciously and in a mutually-respectful way. As your opportunities grow, you can fit your newfound wealth into the framework you developed in the

---

[1] The Law of Attraction can basically be explained by the idea that like attracts like. Like energy, thoughts, and beliefs attract the same energy from the universe and becomes physically manifest in our world. While controversial, there is some science to support it. For more info, see the works of Abraham-Hicks and the 2006 movie, "The Secret."

previous step so that you are saving, budgeting, investing and making wise choices about your newfound abundant wealth.

Amassing wealth is not all there is to life. What good is financial wealth, or any other kind of wealth, if you can't enjoy it? How much can you enjoy wealth alone? Some people feel like little hamsters on a wheel, making money until they drop dead from stress or exhaustion. They have a lot in the bank, but they guard it ferociously. They won't allow anyone (including themselves) a little taste of the fruits from their labors. Is that how you want to be? I'm guessing it doesn't sound attractive. I will share with you ways to avoid this trap so you can enjoy and share your abundant wealth.

Last but certainly not least, you will develop an action plan custom-made for your life situations. You will directly apply the principles from each of the previous chapters of this book. The plan can be helpful both to those who are employed by others as well as people who want to start their own businesses. I have included a part of the action plan for both scenarios. Workshop participants will have an opportunity to share and fine-tune these action plans together. Participants can then keep in touch and create a buddy system to keep each other on track in a gentle, supportive fashion. If you are working alone, I encourage you to buddy up with someone else who also wants to create abundant wealth. Are you ready to start your journey towards wealth? Great! Let's get started!

CHAPTER 1
DEFINING WEALTH AND ABUNDANCE

When you think of wealth and abundance, what typically pops into your head? I want to explore this with you so you know when you have it and when you don't. In this section we will discuss different types of wealth, and how they play into one's sense of well being. However, first I want you to think about your own definition. Before you read the rest of this chapter, please write down what you think of as wealth and abundance. What is your baseline definition, based on what you have previously thought and experienced? Then please read the section that follows this exercise.

Writing Exercise: Your Current Definition of Wealth and Abundance

When you think of wealth, what comes to your mind?

_____

_____

When you think of abundance, what comes to your mind?

_____

_____

What do wealthy people do? What do their lives look like?

___

___

What would your life look like if you had abundant wealth? What would be different from now?

___

___

___

___

I could define wealth and abundance for you based on what the dictionary tells me. Yet I believe there are more subjective values that have a larger influence on how we define both terms. For example, abundance basically means "having a copious quantity of something". You can have abundant cheese on your nachos, or abundant chickenpox. The way it is most often used these days is to describe having a lot of financial wealth. The dictionary definition has been embellished and adapted this way by our current culture in the United States. Similarly, when we say a person has wealth, we most often think about having physical possession of money or resources. Only at the end of the dictionary definition do we find a more general definition, "a plentiful supply of a particular desirable thing" or, an archaic definition of "well-being; prosperity". I tend to favor the latter two definitions of wealth because they are all-encompassing . They also allow for a less materialistic concept of wealth.

I believe there are many different types of wealth, which I will now explain. First I will cover social wealth; then physical health; then emotional and spiritual wealth; and finally, financial wealth. At the end of this explanation, you will do another written exercise to explore your personal definition of wealth. It will be informative to see how this section of the book influences your definition. It will also be interesting to compare this new definition to your baseline definition of wealth.

Social Wealth. You probably have noticed that having friends is important in life. They give you companionship and support. When you're in crisis because your teenager is driving you crazy, you call a friend. Venting about the antics of your son or daughter is priceless. Going to the amusement park can be fun, but if you don't have a friend to share the excitement, it's less fulfilling. Friendships can both sustain us when life is bumpy and stressful, and make life more fun and interesting. Most people don't consider having friends a sign of wealth, but I would argue otherwise. There is even evidence that close friendships can provide protection from illness and premature death.[2] What is more precious than life itself?

Many of us build our lives around our family and friends. Some people are more isolated, while others are rich with friendships. There are many factors that determine a person's ability to have and keep satisfying relationships. There is personality, availability, and comfort with strangers. In the case of teenagers and young people, much of their lives are involved in socializing and having friends. High school and college provide fertile chances for friendships. Having friends is still important when you're an adult, but some people forget that or are unable to achieve lasting friendships. In contrast to adolescents and youngsters, many senior citizens become isolated. They have outlived their spouses and many of their friends. If they have not been actively pursuing and building new friendships over the years, they can find themselves very isolated. Friendships are important at every stage of our lives, whether or not we are aware of their importance.

---

[2] See Karren, K., Hafen, B., Smith, N. and Frandsen, K. (2006). *Mind/Body Health: The Effects of Attitudes, Emotions, and Relationships, 3rd Ed.* San Francisco, CA: Pearson Education, Inc., p. 329.

As we grow older, it's important to remember to keep some of the exuberance of youth, including your excitement over having friends. A true friend will share the good times as well as support you during the difficult times. As we go about our daily lives, we have to remember to keep friendships and other relationships alive. We must make that an equally compelling priority to building financial wealth. In working and starting a family, we have built in social networks. They consist of our family members, spouses, friends, coworkers and bosses. However, what happens if you get sick and can't work, or if you get divorced? It can be difficult to rebuild your social life under such circumstances. It is still important for your emotional and physical well being that you do so. You may need a support group of people going through similar struggles to rebuild after such a loss. Many people who do find it rewarding and worthwhile. I've found in my psychotherapy practice that the tragic loss of family members can be made more bearable by having friends.

At this point I'd like to mention the difference between face to face relationships and computer friendships. I am reminded of the story of the man who had 1,000 friends on Facebook. He decided to give a party and invited them all. No one came. It's not that one doesn't get some social needs fulfilled on the computer. A face to face friendship is much richer, truer and deeper than on social networking sites. As we grow older, it's important to remember to keep some exuberance of youth, including your excitement over having friends. A true friend will share the good times as well as support you during difficult times. Research has shown that the love and support of others is very beneficial to your health.

Physical Health *Is* Wealth. Anyone who has broken a bone, been to the hospital, or been laid up with the flu for a week knows the value of good health. People with chronic health conditions know it even better. When we build our family, work, and social lives, we want to keep our health and it's maintenance in mind. We want to choose our activities and our foods as a way to promote our health. A sound body and mind can help us create the abundance we are trying to reach.

Many people push themselves at work to excel and achieve financial success. Almost all of us spend more time working than we want to. We have to be careful not to sacrifice our health in the process. Many people in their rush to get to work early and not waste time on breakfast, start their days with a coffee and a cigarette. They then expect peak performance from themselves until lunch time. If they just awakened ten minutes earlier, they could at least have some cereal or whole wheat toast, so that their bodies have complex carbohydrates to last them until lunch time. The same principle applies to lunch. A person who takes ten minutes before bedtime to make a lunch salad with low fat dressing on the side has a healthier lunch with more time to enjoy it than the person who rushes to a fast food restaurant. They also spend less money and enjoy more time to digest their food. Studies have shown that a child who eats breakfast before school performs better than one who skips breakfast. Why should we think it is different for an adult?

Another health pitfall from work is stress. Every job has some degree of stress. Finding healthy tools to cope with stress is essential. It's not uncommon for people to wait for the cocktail hour as a way of decompressing from the day's stress. I have found in the past that taking a walk at break time or lunch time (which I always took), helped alleviate some stress. Stretching and other exercise can also help. If I don't have enough time for a walk, I go down a few flights of stairs and back up, just to get my blood moving.

People have their day's work, and then the commute that adds to their stress. Listening to positive thinking tapes, books on tape, and music I love on the way home from work can help ease the day's tension, before arriving home. Some days you might be very hungry and therefore anxious to get home to eat. Keeping snacks with you or in the car can help avoid the stress and discomfort of hunger. If you like sweet snacks, apples, carrots or fruit juice can do the trick. For someone who enjoys salty snacks, nuts, pickles, or cut up vegetables are some healthy alternatives. With a snack, you might come home happier and then eat a lighter dinner. There's also less chance of craving unhealthy processed food. All of these methods can help alleviate stress on the way home.

It is vitally important to leave as much stress as possible at work. I had a job where on my way to the employee parking lot from work, I passed a sign. I imagined as I walked past that sign, there was invisible netting that caught all the stress as I passed through. Between this and a few deep breaths on the way to the car, I began the process of relaxation. I also realized that thinking about the clients and their problems at home did not accomplish much. So I would tell myself, "I'll handle that problem when I get back to work." Then I would worry about remembering to handle the problem. To remedy this, I started to keep a notebook handy to write down all the day's issues. I took it with me in my purse. I would look at it the next morning at work. None of the above ideas is a magic cure. I would still continually remind myself to relax and move away from the worries throughout the course of my evening. If I had a big presentation the next day, I was less stressed using these methods.

Giving myself a breather from work was very important! I was careful to celebrate the fact that I had not thought about the big presentation for over an hour, rather than reprimanding myself for having it come up in my mind again. This made me fresher the next day, so the presentation could go smoother. Exercise also helps with stress and overall physical well being. I found that even with physical labor jobs, I would do better if I went to the gym and did a light workout. Even if I just sat in the hot tub and sauna, I would feel better than just going home and sitting on the couch. If I sat at a desk all day, exercise was even more important. Like most people, I was tired at the end of the day and just wanted to go home. I would repeat to myself, "You know you'll feel better if you go to the gym." This helped motivate me to do what was best for my health. I always felt better after I exercised.

Health is also important to keep in mind during the time you spend with your family. The best way to teach about being healthy is to model it for your children and your partner. Doing healthy activities together is a good way to get everyone in the family into good habits. A friend used to walk with his family every night after dinner. Some nights he claimed he was "too tired", but the kids would cajole him into their usual activity. It helped him enjoy the time with his family. He also modeled a healthy lifestyle for his kids and helped them get used to exercise as a fun, wholesome habit. Even a brief walk is healthier than a 0-minute walk, and as mentioned above, it helps alleviate stress. Another way to enjoy your family and improve your health simultaneously is to spend a day at the pool instead of in front of the TV or the X-box. Everyone learns by doing. The entire family learns how good exercise can be by doing it together.

Physical health for the whole family is enhanced with healthier eating habits. Healthy eating does not have to be a painful process for anyone in the family. Making simple substitutions and cooking at home can help both your physical health and your pocketbook. The same thing applies when going out to dinner. If you encourage your children to eat healthfully, try to pick the healthy choices from the menu for yourself. At home, enlist your children for help in meal preparation and selection, and use this as a chance to educate them about what makes a healthy, balanced meal. If they must eat what everyone else is eating, for example hot dogs, find a healthy substitution such as turkey dogs or tofu dogs. Another simple modification is taking along healthy snacks for yourself and your kids in the car. Fruit, nuts, dried fruit, water, juice, and vegetables all provide a healthy, inexpensive alternative to fast food take-out and quickie-marts.

By weaving choices that support your physical health into your daily life, you are safeguarding one of your most valuable assets: you. You can't make money, travel, and play with your grandkids, etc. if you're substantially unhealthy. It also costs a lot less money to be healthy in the long run than it does to be sick. Think of the costs of going to the doctor, getting surgery, missing work, buying medications, paying higher health insurance premiums, etc. Good health as a preventative medicine that includes exercise and eating healthfully is a lot simpler and less expensive than all that. You can start making healthy choices right now, right here, such choices often don't take huge lifestyle changes to implement. Just imagine how much more you can enjoy your financial wealth if you feel well physically!

Emotional and Spiritual Wealth. We do not get to choose our parents or the early events that shape our lives. We do choose where we go from there, and how we cope with the fallout from past events. We also choose how we view the world. We can decide how to fit into the web of interconnectivity that is human existence.

Have you ever met someone who seemed to have it all, but did not appreciate any of it? No matter what latest toys or cars he or she had, he never felt that he had enough? That person may have had financial abundance, but lacked emotional and spiritual abundance. Without emotional well being and spiritual well being, it's hard to enjoy financial success. A person who does not address the hurtful issues from the past has to work harder to move forward in life.

I have a friend and business associate named Jan. By all outward appearances, she is very successful with her business and owns 10 buildings. However, she does not enjoy the fruits of her success. Instead she is more concerned with collecting more things. Her way of dealing with her psychological issues is hoard things even if she can't afford them. If she does not rent a building right away, she begins to fill it with stuff. She even searches in dumpsters for "valuable items" and brings them back to her buildings. Her sense of gratitude and grace have been impaired by her belief that she doesn't have enough. Her continual gathering of stuff is a way of placating her emotional and spiritual emptiness. No matter how many buildings and how much stuff she has, the emptiness is not filled. This creates a compulsion to acquire more, even at the cost of risking what she has. Jan needs to take the time, courage, and some of her resources to address her emptiness. She would then be emotionally, financially, and spiritually better off.

Mental and spiritual health are important parts of abundance. It is human nature to avoid dwelling on that which is painful or uncomfortable. When something bad happens, we have to keep on living. Otherwise, anger, fear, confusion and pain can easily get buried in our hearts. Unfortunately, sometimes it stays buried, but it still affects us in unexpected and unhealthy ways. It takes discipline and courage to face those parts head-on. The old issues will not block our path to success if we find better ways of handling them. If the issues are not addressed, they will interfere with effective action in the present. I have done psychotherapy with plenty of people whose past issues with authority figures (like parents) obstruct their success with friendships, romantic relationships, and bosses or clients. It is always thrilling to watch people move beyond fear and anger. They are then able to see people in their present lives for who they truly are. They show great courage to put the past behind them by working through it, instead of escaping or avoiding it.

Furthermore, healing emotionally creates a more peaceful and pleasant world for individuals and those around them. By dealing with these issues instead of trying to bury them, we create a more emotionally healthy world within ourselves and surround us. We also clear the pathway for abundance in our lives. Unlike the hoarder mentioned above, we do not allow emotional and physical clutter to get in the way of our abundance. Seeking emotional health through psychological counseling, support groups, workshops, and self-help books can help create a sense of peace and well being that greatly improves your life.

One of the tools that help people move forward is a spiritual belief. This can take the form of believing in God or a higher power, attending your local place of worship, or simply believing in people's goodness. You may also develop a personal meditative practice. Gratitude, a sense of belonging, community, and interconnectedness are some of the traits of spiritual abundance. Whichever path you choose is your own decision. You can be supported through life's daily struggles with the strength you receive through the love of community, the Universe, or God. Spiritual connectivity can make us feel less vulnerable in the world. This strengthens our ability to emotionally bond with other people, which leads to emotional and spiritual abundance.

Financial Wealth. How do you know when you've achieved financial success or wealth? Many people look to the media and American culture to define wealth. They see beautiful cars, homes, clothes, bodies, etcetera as "proof" of their success. I define financial abundance differently. Having financial stability (including savings and being out of debt) makes me feel wealthy. So does the ability to achieve and enjoy things I desire. These are the benchmark of financial success to me. This includes the ability to pay for a new car if I need one, but not buying a new car if I don't need it. To achieve this I make choices that have the bigger picture in mind like a happy working life; and happy retirement. I also avoid debt at all coast, unless it will be worthwhile in the end.

There is debt that is responsible, that works for you in the long run. This includes a home mortgage, student loans, or a small business loan (provided you can pay it back). These types of debt are building blocks to a greater future. However, going into debt to satisfy fleeting impulses is not as responsible. Such debt can create unhealthy spending habits that can be difficult to reverse. What is more stressful, doing repairs on an old car to make it last, or buying a new car and having to make car payments every month? These payments would strain your budget for the next five years. Instead, if you saved that car payment in a bank account for the next three and a half years you could buy that same car without paying the interest. If you have to use that money, it's in the bank for an emergency, not tied up in a pretty car. You do not lose your car to repossession because an emergency cost you what you'd saved for the car payment. You simply modify your savings plan and take the money out of the bank. This is just one example of how you can modify your expenses in the short run and have more money in the long run. By saving for purchases in advance, you save on interest as well as having the comfort of money in the bank. This keeps you from living on the edge.

If you are in debt, your efforts should be to cut down on spending and paying down your debt. You should always have some money in savings for emergencies, but it doesn't make sense to have too much money owed on your credit card while having a lot of money in savings. You are not just in debt for the amount owed for your purchase. There is also interest on the credit card, which can be 12-29%. It is the same with student loans. The loans have lower interest, but you still pay interest. If you can afford to make double payments on your student loan, and your loans are for a 10 year period, you save roughly 30% in interest. You can save that money for building your financial future. Debt creates stress whether you realize it consciously or not. You must ask yourself if the stress created by your debt is worth what you're purchasing before you buy it. if it is necessary then pay down the debts as quickly as possible, to avoid continuing to pay interest.

Saving is a way to have security and not have to worry about money when big expenses come up. Having this without debt is quite an achievement for many people. It's not a sign of failure to live within your means and not buy the latest toys for your kids or the latest gadgets for yourself. It's a sign of success to have fewer gadgets and more money in the bank.

This is not to say that you should only save and be miserable. It's fun to go on vacation and buy things that you like. You can still do that, but in moderation and with the bigger picture in mind. When you dream of what you want to do, dream big. We all have the right to dream big. Just know the difference between your fantasy and reality. The financial difference has to be made up somehow. How will you make that difference, and what impact will that have on your future? We all have the right to dream big. If it takes me ten years to achieve a dream vacation that I can pay for out of pocket, I savor the dream longer and enjoy it more. This is cheaper and less stressful than putting it on a credit card. I would then pay for the trip, pay the interest, and carry the stress of a high credit card balance. I can have what I want financially, I just need to be realistic about it.

Mere financial independence or success is not enough. I strive to direct[3] energy and effort toward all these areas so that my life is meaningful and enjoyable. I want the life I create to give me a sense of being loved and capable as well as security. I recognize that I am not everyone. I am just me. I'm curious to know what you think is a successful life is? As you read through these definitions, what has attracted your attention the most? Think about what jumped out at you as most desirable now, and why. If you can describe your bigger picture, the reason for your taking this course in the first place, then you're on your way to defining wealth and abundance for yourself.

---

[3] The author James Arthur Ray, in his video called "Harmonic Wealth," makes a really good point about having balance in one's life versus harmony. He says that balance is a static condition and that we can't achieve that because of the dynamic nature of life. Instead, we can strive to have harmony in all areas of our lives so that they work together in creating a symphony. This harmony allows us to grow with the expanding universe and enjoy all aspects of life.

Writing Exercise on Defining Abundance, Part II:

1. What is your current definition of wealth and abundance?

_____

_____

2. Which types of wealth are most important to you? Why?

_____

_____

3. Read what you originally wrote about the definitions of wealth and abundance. Do you see a change in how defined it then versus now? What changed about your view?

_____

_____

4. What internal resistance do you have to wealth in all areas of your life?

_____

_____

Later we will look at resistance to abundant wealth more deeply. Right now we are charting the course for the journey to abundant wealth. Later we will work through the obstacles to the flow of wealth in your life.

CHAPTER 2
EXAMINING YOUR BELIEFS ON THE
CURRENT TIDES OF WEALTH

Beliefs about money are like currents in a river. They channel the flow of money into and out of your life. You can change the course of them by becoming conscious of blocking beliefs. With your new consciousness you can change those beliefs that hinder your progress. If you imagine a river with a layer of money floating on top, most people see their jobs as a way to scoop some of that money as it flows by. What we will learn through this book is how to create a way to divert some of that money into a reservoir so that you are not working to scoop money for the rest of your life. That way, in times of drought, you have a reserve to utilize for basic necessities as well as things you want.

The first step in changing the current is recognizing what the current is. A current is a pattern of thought and behavior that recurs in your life. A friend of mine named Ralph was always helping his friends by lending them money. He was truly a warm-hearted, generous individual. If he had money saved and a friend approached him, Ralph would be the first person to lend them money. However, when Ralph needed money for his own financial droughts, the friends rarely were able to pay him back. He found that when he pressed the friends for money, he not only had lost his money, but he also lost the friendships. He leant the money because he wanted to be a nice person and help his friends. However, when it came to asking for the money back, he was afraid of losing their approval. It had been his experience that when he asked for repayment of the loan the people generally didn't have it or resented him for asking for it. Usually it harmed the friendships.

When Ralph examined his beliefs about lending, he saw that he chose to lend to friends who he knew were unlikely to pay him back. The pattern indicated that he believed that he should give more than he should receive. He saw that by lending the money he lost more friends then he kept or gained. His need to lend or rather give reflected his own low self esteem. He realized that he was lending money for approval, and that ultimately people were disapproving of him instead. Thus, he decided that this current was not working for him. Once he understood how to control the flow of his money, he no longer lent the money as he did before. This way, he kept his worthwhile friends and had money when he needed it.

Part of what Ralph learned was that he was worthy of having abundance in his life. I feel that we are all worthy of having abundance. However, we have to learn how to believe that and make our beliefs come true. Ralph was scooping up money at his job and putting it into the pocket of his friends. He was rerouting the money that he needed to other people, and wondering why the financial flow wasn't headed towards him. He had some issues to deal with. Nonetheless, he was open to self examination, honesty and trying new thoughts and behaviors. This changed the flow of his abundance. He also stopped surrounding himself with people who took advantage of his need for approval. They were obviously not quality friends. After he addressed his low self esteem, he realized he was worthy of abundance, it helped him direct more cash flow into his financial reservoir, where he could use it for his own emergency needs as well as building more wealth.

Here are some questions that he answered in order to identify his currents about money.

- What financial situations do you find yourself in repeatedly? What are the beliefs behind these situations?

_____

_____

_____

- Are you worthy of having abundant wealth? Some people say "yeah, but..." Do you have "yeah buts" about your worthiness of wealth?

_____

_____

_____

(If you don't feel worthy, we can help you remove the barriers to feeling worthy. Just by being here, there must be some part that believes it's possible.)

- What is the part of you that resists? Describe that resistance to yourself, and if you feel like it, tell trusted others.

_____

_____

_____

I hope that by examining your definition of wealth and abundance, you can have a clearer picture of what you want. It's important to have a clear target, so you can prepare your mind for receiving more wealth. In the next section, you can now examine your beliefs about abundance and see how they materialize into your financial situation.

Charting and Challenging Your Beliefs about Your Job, Yourself and Money

I suggest that you chart your beliefs about yourself, your job, and your money on a log. Make a separate log for each one so it doesn't get confusing for you. In one column, write down the thought that you had. In the next column, write down what happened just before you had that thought. For example, "talked to my boss about a raise" or "got a new client on the phone". That column is called, "Precipitating event."

Next, circle the thoughts that you have the most often. Try to make a note on the chart which ones feel good to think (I would abbreviate that as FG for feel good) and which ones don't feel good (DFG). Then try to figure out why the DFG items don't feel good to you. In the "origin" column, write down where you got that belief. Was it something your mom and dad said, or is it from the media? Did it come from personal experiences you've had with certain people or gaining or losing money? It's interesting to see what patterns you've learned and whether you compare yourself to others with less or more money than you. Finally, think about how this belief could be changed so that it makes you feel good. By that I mean hopeful, motivated, healthy, etc. Write this in the last column that reads, "New Thought." There are many interesting questions to consider when doing this project. I am inserting a sample form to use; you can change it any way you like to suit your own exploration.

Lisa S. Larsen, PsyD

Charting and Challenging Your Thoughts About Money Form

© 2010 Lisa S. Larsen

Thought	Precipitating event	FG/DFG	Origin	New thought

It's also important to consider whether you believe that what you have defines you as a person (i.e.," I drive a nice car so I must be superior "or "I have a big house so I must be successful"). Is having more important than being? We've all met people who turn up their noses at other people who have less than they do, or who feel anxious if they don't have the latest, best gadget or the nicest dress or car. Such people seem to confuse style for substance, and are often chronically dissatisfied with what they have or what they are, because it could always be better. Those people appear to prioritize having objects over being happy and peaceful. Such financial currents can create a trap that we find ourselves in when we get too caught up in possession of wealth.

Finally, look at what thought comes up most frequently when you think about wealth. That is your governing principle. If it's not positive and affirming, then it's a good idea to change it now. How to do this? Critically evaluate your beliefs. How true is the belief? What proof do you have for this idea? Consider next who told you to believe this way. Is it something your parents always said, or that you saw on television, or that friends often said? Why do you think other people want you to think this? What's in it for them? Where did your beliefs originate? What environment helped create your beliefs? Have you observed this belief in action in your life? Is there another possible explanation for what you think you observed?

Perhaps most importantly, you need to ask: How does this belief serve me? Sometimes there is a hidden gain even from the most torturous, self-limiting ideas. Some of the beliefs keep us safe. Other ideas let us off the hook for trying harder or absolve us of responsibility. This can be hard to identify at first but it is worth trying anyway. These are some of the dams that keep the flow of money from coming to you. If it's not helping the flow, you need to consider the cost of holding onto your beliefs. You need to evaluate whether having these beliefs is worth not being where you want to be. For example, you might think that money begets money and if you don't start out rich you'll never get there. Therefore you might as well indulge yourself by purchasing a series of small luxury items.

Have you ever met somebody who is in debt and is having trouble making their basic bills? Yet this same person is the first to get a flat-screened television or always has the latest IPod. Have you seen someone who is about to lose their home to foreclosure but takes a two week vacation to Maui? Such people have accepted what they consider the "fact" that they won't be homeowners or investors. Yet they still want to enjoy the lifestyle of someone more successful than they actually are. They did not divert any of the flow of money into their reservoir, but are rushing to skim their little pile off the top every week. Some people go so far as to go into debt so they can keep buying all these small luxuries. How far are they willing to go? Will they drain their reservoir or lose their homes in order to hold onto this belief? What are your beliefs costing you?

Many people have lost their jobs and then their homes in this economy. Some were seduced by credit cards and ended up paying thousands of dollars in interest. This can be disheartening and very challenging. However, it does not mean that we should give up the fight to live with wisdom and integrity. Having a reservoir of funds does not guarantee that you will find a job right away, but it does allow you to afford to pay your bills and keep your home for awhile as you look for a job.

Let's say two people lost their jobs at the same time. They both had a reservoir in the form of a bank account. Cassie believed that since she was on a sinking financial ship anyway, she might as well drain her reservoir and go into debt to buy cell phones, a new car, etc. Cassie's mindset was, "live for today". She did enjoy today but she regretted it tomorrow. Tanya, however, stopped all her spending aside from the basic necessities (e.g., food, rent and utilities). Tanya stopped dining out, didn't replace her broken DVD player, and focused all her efforts on looking for a job. She believed that things would get better, but only with patience and hard work. When Cassie and Tanya both got another job at roughly the same time, Tanya was left with a little bit in her financial reservoir because she believed things would get better. Cassie, however, had to climb out of debt because she didn't believe things would get better. She thought she might as well have fun while she could. Both people's beliefs created the world they ended up living in.

When we examine unhealthy or unproductive beliefs, we need to replace them with something that does work. Sometimes changing the wording of the belief is all that is needed to create an affirming, supportive belief. Affirmations are useful to replace unhealthy beliefs. Basically an affirmation is something that you say to yourself to declare what you want to have happen in your life. It's a way of taking charge of your destiny, even in a small way by stating your desires. It is also helpful to notice when you feel unhappy about money and trace back what thoughts accompany or came before this feeling. Where in your body do you experience this bad feeling? Once you identify the negative belief/experience, try questioning it or countering it with something more realistic or positive. See how it changes your emotions and actions. When you learn how to identify negative patterns, you can neutralize them or alter them. You gain more power over them. Eventually, the thought patterns you want are stronger currents than the ones you don't want; they gain strength and frequency. They become the dominant currents. When an old negative thought comes along, you know how to challenge and redirect it so it doesn't block the flow.

For instance, if I feel a sense of dread and panic when I open the mail because I'm worried about encountering bills or even collection agencies, that is a cue to me for me to identify the beliefs that are creating that situation. What thought leads to my delinquent bills? Maybe I think if I pay them then I won't have money for fun things, so I'd rather ignore them. Then I can enjoy what I like. What thought do I have about bills in general? Do you resent, or feel disempowered or victimized by them? Do you have any memories of your parents' approach to bill paying? Do you like evading responsibility or getting over on the bill collector? Do you enjoy paying bills on time? These are all important things to pay attention to, as these unprocessed memories may still impact your life and make you uncomfortable at best, or feel impoverished or threatened at worst.

I believe it's also important to think critically about your beliefs about the abundance or scarcity of wealth in the world. Money, energy, love, commerce – all these entities are shared among human beings across the planet. If we resent, pity, hate, fear, or devalue others, even on a subconscious level, it can make it hard to do business with them and to give and receive money, love and energy. If you resent or have contempt for your customers, they will notice it. So will your boss or coworkers. I once knew a young man who resented all authority figures because he had a negative experience with his mother; he was good at getting jobs, but didn't keep them for long. Furthermore, he never had any good references because he found ways to sabotage work projects. He thought he was "getting over on the man," but he was also shooting himself in the foot. He also thought that wealthy people were all conceited jerks, and stayed underemployed for many years without advancing in his career. His beliefs were dams in the flow of his abundance, and since he never took the time to examine them, they tragically kept him from a happier existence.

I'd like to ask you about some of the possible beliefs and attitudes in this area:

- Do you compare yourself to other people and judge them for having more or less than you?

_____

- Do you feel that there is enough wealth to go around?

_____

- How do you honestly feel about others' wealth?

_____

- How do you honestly feel about others' poverty?

_____

- Can you accept what others have and what you have? Is it possible for you to know that there is room for change in both your lives and others' lives?

_____

- What destructive habit are you ready to give up so that you and others can have abundant wealth?

_____

At this point I want to make it clear that I'm not only talking about fiscal abundance, but emotional, spiritual, and social abundance as well. Some of the financially wealthiest people I have met live emotionally impoverished, lonely lives. When we are creating a successful life, we want emotional as well as financial abundance. We want to be gracious and be able to sleep well at night. There was once a real estate agent named Anne who owned many properties. She would buy dilapidated homes and resell them to contractors who could not afford the home. She would work out cheap payments so they could move in. The one stipulation was a large balloon payment two years into the contract. The contractors would move in, fix up the homes, and generally make steady payments. When the balloon payment was due, the payment had been structured to be too expensive for that particular contractor. Contractors would lose the houses because the big balloon payment was too much for their budget. Anne ended up getting the house back, all fixed up. She became very wealthy financially, but very lonely because what she was doing was morally bankrupt and intentionally cruel.

When money becomes the end rather than a means to an end, it can disrupt the harmony of a person's life. Such money lust can occlude the other types of abundant wealth. These stories of rich people exploiting others can make the idea of becoming wealthy unattractive. How many people admire Bernie Madoff, or the CEO at Enron? One doesn't necessarily become evil or exploitive because they have money. The beliefs that the person holds about money shape their behaviors and thus destiny. Being financially wealthy isn't necessarily evil, but corrupting one's moral sense to become wealthy is. Unlike the real estate agent, if you take your time and/or money to help your community and your family, your wealth can extend into love and friendship, as well as spiritual wealth.

What is your attitude about people who have less than you? Do you feel like they deserve what they have? Do you think that they are just lazy, or under-educated, or never had the chances that the rich person had? It is easy to fall into the trap of buying small luxuries if you see yourself or poor people as simply a victim with no chance of overcoming one's circumstances. You may believe that you'll never afford the big ticket items like your own house or even being out of debt. If you allow yourself to fall into the mindset of "I might as well enjoy life as I ruin my credit", like Cassie mentioned above, you become trapped. Feeling victimized because you don't have as much as others can make you feel depressed about trying to change your circumstances. You might think "I'm only capable of surviving" and never try to get more education or job training, or ask for a raise or promotion at work. You help create stagnation or a dam in the flow of abundance to your life. If you allow others' pity or disdain of you to affect your feeling of worthiness, you are allowing those emotions and currents to control your life. If you feel like you are shorted in life, look to the areas where you are rich. Do you have an abundance of friendship, love of your family, health? Does your faith bring beauty or meaning into your life? If you have disdain or a sense of superiority over those who have less, then unfortunately you are missing out on our interconnectedness as human beings. What you have could disappear tomorrow. How will you still love yourself if what you have is who you believe you are?

There are many sayings floating around about the middle class, such as the idea that we are hard working, honest folk who get exploited both by wealthy and poor people alike. Whether you identify as middle class, rich or poor, how you view yourself and others raises some questions about how you think you can survive in the world. Do you think that poor people look up to you, and rich people look down on you? It is interesting to wonder what it means to us to be middle class, poor or wealthy. Do you feel like you deserve your socioeconomic class? Do you see yourself as fortunate or unfortunate?

Sometimes people think that if you are poor or middle class, you don't need or want to donate to charity. However, sometimes people of lower income donate more to charity than people who are wealthy. For example, people who work for one famous big box store make so little that they often receive welfare, and yet give proportionately more of their income to charity than the owners of the company for whom they work. Consider also one very happy middle class person who has spent years saving as well as making small efforts to help his community. He has slowly built a sound fiscal reservoir at the same time as raising a loving, happy family. He taught his children to save as well as help the community. At Christmas time, he and his family adopt a low income family and shop for gifts for that family. At the same time, he does charitable things that take time rather than money, like helping his elderly neighbor clean her yard or shoveling the snow from her front walk. These things provide him a sense of satisfaction as well as friendship. I consider him to be abundant in many ways even though he considers himself "just middle class".

Now that you have started to dig deeper into the thoughts and feelings, that effect our financial currents I would like to discuss two attitudes that people can have about abundance. They are faith and discouragement. These currents can create conduits and dams in the flow of financial abundance.

Faith and Discouragement.

Faith is a terrific antidote to stress. It is the belief that things will be better even when a situation seems hopeless. Faith helps you believe that the right things happen at the right time. It helps you realize that there's a light at the end of the tunnel. People ask me how to have blind faith like this. I tell them that sometimes you have to fake it until you make it. You operate as though things will get better, which gives you the edge of a more joyful , confident attitude towards life. That can lead to being a more charismatic and desirable person, which could translate into having more friendships, job contacts, and optimism. It has been shown that a good attitude helps with healing and wellness[4]. Believing in a power greater than oneself has given faith to many people, as well as confidence in tackling difficult life situations. Quite often people find their faith in a spiritual fellowship like a church, temple or mosque. Their faith helps them believe that a higher power takes care of whatever problem or issues they have, which can ease stress and bolster their resolve to do what they need to do. Some believe that praying leads to being blessed or uplifted from turmoil, by their higher power. Faith found from spirituality and religious beliefs can be very helpful to its adherents.

A person can also have a self-fulfilling prophecy with a good attitude, by going through your day with a smile on ones face. Acting as if things will work out can safeguard oneself from negative thinking. As discussed before you need to notice when you doubt yourself or your life. When you do, you can replace those thoughts with beliefs that you will be all right. Just as with action and follow

---

[4] See Karren, et al.

through, cultivating faith can take hard work and discipline to develop, but the rewards usually prove worthwhile. You cannot do anything in life, without taking positive action to help yourself get out of the tight spot. Therefore, it is best to combine faith with considered action.

Some people think that having faith alone will solve their financial issues. They are not willing or motivated to take concrete actions to advance their goals. When people first learned about the Law of Attraction through the movie, "The Secret", there was much excitement and also skepticism on the part of people who heard about it. The movie suggested that by simply expecting that you would have something desirable or undesirable, it would manifest itself in the material realm. That would be very nice if that were true, but anyone who has ever bought a lotto ticket expecting to win, can tell you that it doesn't necessarily work that way. It's understandable to want the world to operate this way: I expect to have it, so it will come to me, without having to work at it or follow through.

It can take a lot of hard work to turn your dreams into reality. I am somewhere between the true believers and the skeptics. I believe that faith opens the door, but the hard work and action enables you to walk through the door. For example, many people want the magic advertising vehicle that will bring hundreds of new customers into their businesses. I tried such an advertising scheme, but found that the promises made by the advertising company did not pay off for the money and effort I invested. I had to change how I attracted new customers. I found that cold calling other professionals helped bring in new clients, where ad words on search engines did very little to promote my business. People often tell me that they do not like cold calling. This is no surprise to me, as I find it slightly embarrassing to do. I get through it by reminding myself that it works. I have faith that someone will want to refer their patients to me. So far it has paid off a hundred fold compared to paying for internet advertising. I dream big, but take big action to support my dreams too.

We've already discussed how change in one's current state or behavior starts with altering one's thoughts. Faith helps provide the engine to drive those thoughts to reality. Affirmations can be a way to fake it until you make it, at least in your mind. Affirmations are statements that describe how you want your life to be. In order to be effective, they are best stated in the positive and in the present. For example, if I want to lose weight, I don't say, "I am not fat anymore" or "I will lose weight." Instead I say, "I now am the perfect healthy weight for me." If I want to be debt-free, I don't say, "I don't have debt anymore," I would say, "I am financially solvent and all my bills are paid up to date." Take time to ponder the actions that are required to make these statements true, and do something every day to move closer to that reality. Let them guide your behavior and thought patterns as well. If I want to be less judgmental, I don't just say the affirmation "I am accepting of myself, others, and the world as we are." I refrain from making critical or judgmental statements about other people, and I catch myself rushing to categorize things in my world as good or bad. Just like going to school, you don't graduate in one day or pass your classes without daily, sustained effort. So too you must put the time and energy into acting upon your affirmations to make them real.

It's important to have faith in your affirmations. Try to imagine that you already have it and feel the emotions that you would have if you achieved your goal. You might not have what you want now, but you need to believe that it will come in time. It is like working in your garden. When you put a seed in dirt, you don't have a plant right away. You simply have something underground that is supposed to become a plant. You water it and nurture it with the faith that it will become a plant. Beliefs are like this. What beliefs are you watering in your head? If you believe that there is only financial wealth or that you will never own your own home, this will foster manifesting those beliefs into reality. In other words, make sure you're not watering and nurturing negative beliefs. Like weeds, negative beliefs can flourish unchecked and take over; therefore, you want to nurture beliefs that will feed your faith and blossom into a beautiful reality.

One way to develop faith includes focusing on your past successes to bolster your belief in your ability to be successful again. Think about when you have felt powerful, successful, and in control of your life and your money. Sometimes we have big successes. We can take the memory and energy of those successes and use them to bolster our self confidence. If you're just starting out or have had what you think are only failures, then focus on areas of your life that have been positive or successful. It doesn't have to be about financial success. Maybe you changed an old pattern from your family of origin that helped you parent your children better. You became the parented that you wanted, not the one you had. Perhaps you created a satisfying social life with close, loving relationships with your family and friends. You might have raised money for your church or favorite charity, or given a speech for your volunteer group that inspired people. Even passing grade school or graduating from high school can be seen as a series of small successes. One of the ways to build yourself up is by mentally listing these successes: I married a wonderful woman; I support my family; I have raised wonderful children; I controlled my temper when my daughter said she wanted to start dating. Take the time to congratulate yourself for these small and large successes. It can leave you with the feeling that you are doing better than you previously thought. This can bolster your faith and increase your sense of what is possible. This sense of success can motivate you toward your future goals.

Another way to increase your energy around faith is to focus on the desirable part of your goal. How will your life be different when you have abundance? You could even draw a picture or make a collage of what you want to have in your life and put it somewhere that you see regularly. Think of how much you will enjoy living the reality portrayed on your success collage. Try to involve as many sensory cues as possible: what will you see, smell, hear, taste, and feel when you have achieved abundance? Focus on those feelings every day before or after work. We all create the reality we live in, and this is a way to create a reality where you achieve your goals successfully. It can be a searchlight when you're in the fog of despair or discouragement.

The flip side of faith is discouragement. Sometimes you will do everything you think is right and still not get the results you want. At this point it's easy to think "all this positive thinking is a bunch of hooey" and give up, even for a day. Try to keep a good attitude and your faith even at these times. For example, there are two guys on a life raft adrift in the middle of the ocean. A life raft has two chambers that hold air, one on either side of the raft. One of the chambers pops and deflates, but the other chamber is still intact. One guy says, "We're stuck on a life raft in the middle of the ocean, and now, we're going to drown." The other one smiles and says, "Thank goodness there is still another chamber!" When they do get saved, the one guy tells his rescuers, "I thought you'd never get here, what took you so long?" The other man thanks his rescuers for coming to their aid.

The first man's negative attitude made the ordeal more stressful, for a number of reasons. The man with optimism and gratitude was still concerned but did not make a bad situation worse in his mind. When your plans don't work out as you'd hoped, you can either make one of two choices. You can be the person who decides "this is the end," or you can be the person who sees this as an opportunity to start afresh. You can take the lessons of your misfortune and move forward. Considering the circumstances, the man who thought life was ending had a certain amount of logic, but he made life miserable for himself while he waited for rescue. The man with the faith created a better life for himself moment-by-moment, including the day in the middle of the ocean.

One way to overcome discouragement is to keep an open mind and attitude toward what life and the universe offers you. Sometimes it gives you what you want in disguise. It can give you the key to get what you want but you have to take more steps to get it. Most of us follow a winding path toward what we end up doing with our lives. The reason that colleges have general education classes is that people don't always know which career direction they will take. They might start out in one field and wind up falling in love with another. They could find out that what they want to do is not practical or as lucrative as they imagined. You might start your education wanting a better job and wind up with a career that helps people. Having many lawyers in my family, I began college thinking of becoming a lawyer. After I completed my BA with a major in legal studies and literature, I realized that what I liked about the law was helping people. This left many other professions and career paths open to me. While I didn't become Chief Justice of the Supreme Court, I took my opportunity to excel in other ways. Now I get to help people every day in my job, and I feel an extreme satisfaction with what I do because of that. I followed my heart to a life I love, but it took me on some interesting detours!

Another way to banish discouragement is to find what inspires you and gets you out of a funk. Is there a song, prayer or activity that you find uplifting? Perhaps this is a time when you can make a list of things that lift you up, including a list of your successes. I have a friend who has written down all her life's big and small successes in her life. When things become dark for her, she simply reads this list to herself and it perks her up. How do you think it would be to consider all the successes you've had in your life?

Writing exercise: Tell of a time when you overcame internal and external obstacles to get what you wanted. What specifically did you do and think to achieve this?

_____

_____

_____

_____

Creating and Practicing Affirmations for Abundance

Affirmations are a way to state, sort out, or assert something. They make your beliefs grow stronger in your mind, thus crowding out your unhealthy thoughts about abundance. Take the limiting beliefs about yourself and others and turn them into positive affirmations. For example, if you think you will never have what you want, change that to an affirmation that says "I have all that I could ever want in life." The affirmations create a different mindset that turns your actions toward your true intentions. If you are having trouble saving your money, create an affirmation that tells yourself you will take a certain percentage of your salary and put it into savings every pay day. If you're in tight financial straits but want to help your affirmations become a reality, save one percent of your income. That is only one dollar for every 100 dollars you make. That way, you have started a habit of acting in accordance with your affirmation. You structured your life to create success.

Add affirmations to the beliefs that seem to work for you. For example, if I believe that God will provide, simply amend that belief by saying "I help God provide." Just saying this can make you feel more empowered. You have yourself and your higher power's energy working together. Take your healthy beliefs that you have unearthed from the previous chapter and incorporate those into the affirmations as well. Some examples of my affirmations are, "I am 100% happy, healthy and prosperous;" "I always get exactly what I want, and I always have plenty of money;" and "I have abundance in all areas of my life." These always lift me up even if they do not become manifest immediately.

Practice these daily in the morning to get you revved up for the day. Say them with conviction and exercise patience with their fruition. Please don't be disappointed that all your affirmations don't come true the first day. Having faith daily that things will work out eventually becomes reality. Many people lose patience and give up on their affirmations before they have a chance to become habitual and programmed into your mindset. Simply saying the affirmations daily is an expression of faith and encourages one to believe in their dreams. My affirmations change, and this keeps me in touch with my changing goals and dreams. Affirmations help kept me going in the right direction.

When I don't do my affirmations, I don't have as much faith and direction in my day. I lack energy and commitment to my goals, and sometimes I get bogged down in an unproductive attitude. The affirmations cheer me up; they give me hope that I will achieve what I want. Without that hope, it's hard to sustain all the activities and stressors that go into running a business and working hard. If I find that I am grumpy from not doing my affirmations, I try to identify things in my life for which I'm grateful. This can change my attitude for the better. It doesn't take that long to do the affirmations, but I miss them and lose productive time if I don't take those few minutes each day.

If you have trouble generating your own affirmations, you can check out Chellie Campbell's book *The Wealthy Spirit*. Many of my initial affirmations came directly from her books. I like to adjust them for my own purposes, but it's a good place to get started. Try to have affirmations for all types of wealth, not just financial. That way you can build life where all types of wealth are in harmony with one another. This can lead to true success and happiness.

There are some guidelines that can make affirmations more effective. They should be stated in the present tense, name what you want, and specify that in the positive. For example, I don't want to say, "I don't want to be in debt anymore" because the mind doesn't hear negatives like "don't". Instead one might say "I am financially solvent and secure." The same goes for the other areas of abundance. If you want more friends, you could say "I have many wonderful friends in my life." You do not want to say "I am lonely". Remember that the mind only hears the positive.

If you feel silly doing affirmations, ask yourself whether it's worth feeling silly for a bit to improve your life. If your family or roommates get on your case about it, do it in private. Create some "me" time in front of the mirror and say them aloud. Play around with them and laugh. Do them in traffic as a way of seizing the moment and distracting yourself from the guy in front of you. Have fun! What harm can feeling silly do? Believe (or try to believe) that they empower you and help you accomplish your goals. Affirmations and positive thinking set the stage for greater abundance. However if you don't know how to manage the money you have they are not sufficient alone to sustain and build wealth. The next section helps with the nuts and bolts of handling money.

CHAPTER 3
EDUCATING YOURSELF ABOUT MONEY AND ITS PROPER MANAGEMENT

In order to manage money well, we have to become educated about available options for savings, investment, and debt reduction. In this section, we will discuss savings, debt reduction, compulsive spending and, investment. This will give you basic guidelines for each topic.

Creating a reservoir or increasing your existing one

Goal one is creating a small cushion, or reservoir, in the bank. Once you have done that, you can pay down debt. This often starts by plugging some holes in your dam to keep your cash from flowing away so quickly. Like any change, the first step is awareness. You need to become aware of where your money goes. This involves keeping track of where your money goes in relation to your income, otherwise known as a budget. Create a simple set of categories, like health, food, transportation, home; school; miscellaneous; and entertainment. As you spend, save the receipt from each thing you buy in your wallet and write it down when you get home. Think of what you spend money on each week; what comes to your mind first? These are the categories to include in your budget, and can be unique to your particular lifestyle. Total each category at the end of the month and see how it measures against your income. The total of expenditures should be smaller than your income.

Also note what you paid for outright and what you put on a credit card. I put the credit card in the correct column, but in red ink. If I add up the red figures I know what I owe on my credit card. When you total it up your expenses in each category should be added up separately and then all the subtotals should be added together. The purpose of this is not to make you feel cheap or shamed, but merely aware of how your money is being spent. You can see how much of your income goes to each category. Perhaps you will become enlightened about spending habits that you never knew existed. With that knowledge comes the power to change.

Some people can look at the totals and see most of their money is going to entertainment, for example. Other people break down the percentages and make a pie chart to see where things are going. If I look at my budget and see that I spend $500 per month on entertainment, I could decide to reduce that amount by choosing a reasonable amount for me. Dividing that amount by 4.3 weeks that are in the average month lets me know how much I can spend per week on entertainment. If I want to do an activity that is over the amount I want to spend, I don't dip into next week's money. Instead, I save this week's money so I can do that activity next week. This makes my entertainment decisions simpler. I have gone from awareness of an idea to enacting an idea, which is how we make all changes in our lives. These small changes multiply up to big savings over time. If I cut my $500 budget for entertainment down to $250, and I save the difference, I have $3,000 more in savings by the end of the year.

Here are some other small things to save on that add up:
- Bringing a bagged lunch to work more often than eating out;
- Eating out at a cheaper restaurant than an expensive one;
- Bringing your coffee to work instead of getting it at a local coffee store;

- Allowing yourself one meal out per week or month, not to be exceeded;
- Using cash instead of checks or debit cards;
- Setting aside a portion of your income (the common wisdom is at least 10%) each month to a savings account; and waiting for nonessential items to go on sale before purchasing them. You could then use *some* of that saved amount to buy what you want for less!

Also, if you can make something easily for cheaper than buying it pre made, then make it rather than buy it. I drink cactus pear juice twice a day for my health, and I save substantially by purchasing the pears myself and juicing them at home than I would if I ordered a similar prepared drink from a company that makes a similar drink. Besides, I get a nicer pure cactus juice when I make it myself. All the money we save from our daily decisions helps build our reservoir, little by little.

Once I understand where my money is going, I can make informed decisions on how to save it. If I go back to the example above, a person who cut their entertainment spending has created a $3,000 financial reservoir in one year. Assuming this person had no savings before, this gives them a little cushion for life's surprises. Having a reservoir can be useful but if there are leaks in it, like interest on debt, it may be harder to keep this reservoir filled for the future.

When you spend money for an emergency, it's important to define an "emergency" carefully and realistically. If someone in your family is in a car crash and needs you to stay with them at the hospital, that's pretty clearly an emergency. However, some people use the term more loosely. Let me assure you that an opportunity to buy a property that you want that seems "once in a lifetime" is probably not an emergency. Feeling upset and needing to do "retail therapy" is also not an emergency. You may unwittingly use the term to rationalize spending thoughtlessly.

People also use the term "have to" to describe expenses. Often what they "have to" spend money on is not as essential to their existence as they think. Do you "have to" buy an iPod for your kid? Do you "have to" have cable TV? Is it possible that you use this to justify nonessential expenses? One thing to ask yourself about such circumstances is, "what would happen if I didn't spend this money?" You might write down all the possible things that could happen, good or bad, if you didn't spend that money. That might help clarify whether it's truly life or death, or whether something else could be done to help the situation. Are you one of those big-hearted individuals who gives people what they want, without a second thought? Beware of this tendency, as people can manipulate you with that word, "emergency." Then your loyalty or love for them may cloud your ability to objectively see whether it's truly an emergency that requires you to use your savings.

Plugging up the Dam

Remember how we talked about responsible debt versus irresponsible debt? Chronologically, the first debt most people incur is student debt. An education is important, and this is an investment that pays for itself in greater wages and later a career that you enjoy. It is important to choose a career that will give you pleasure and purpose, as well as one that might enable you to pay back your student loans. For example, a doctor or lawyer might be able to afford to incur more student debt (and often does), than an artist or philosopher. However an artist or philosopher may have less stress and more of the other kinds of wealth in their lives. Try to incur as little debt as possible while you're going to school. If you qualify for student loans, it doesn't necessarily mean you have to take every penny they offer. Think hard about what bare essentials you need while in school. Don't travel to Italy or invest in the stock market with your student loan money. It's just there to pay for school and living expenses and nothing else.

Similarly with a mortgage, don't buy a house that costs more per month than you can afford. Ask your bank many questions about how much you will wind up paying in interest as well as principal, and whether balloon payments are involved in the mortgage they offer. For many years, a maximum of one third of your income was the standard rule of thumb for your mortgage payment or rent payment. Even if a real estate agent or banker tells you differently. Do the math for yourself. Don't get into a situation where you could lose the house through missed payments by trying to buy a house that is too expensive for you. These missed payments can lead to foreclosure.

When paying down debt, use the same formula mentioned above. Break down the categories and see where the greatest amount is showing up in your debt. Also check which debt has the highest interest. Then try to reduce how much you spend on those categories. The most expensive debt people carry is credit cards. As we all know, there is a minimum payment to make on a credit card, which is a small percentage of the total owed. Ideally, you should pay off the full balance each month. When I use my credit card, I save my receipts and I account for it in my budget the day I used it. This helps me be aware that the amount I owe on the credit card is money actually coming out of my pocket. It is not some abstract number that I can pretend I don't have to repay. I write credit card expenditures in red so I can glance at my budget and see what my next credit card bill will be so it is not a surprise. This helps me to be able to pay my full balance each month.

You are starting with awareness of where the credit card purchases are most heavy. If you want to make the minimum payment on your credit card, since that is all you can afford, then try to make yourself aware of what the consequences are of making the minimum payment. What is the interest rate? How much is the interest on your current balance costing you? When and how will you pay that off? If you multiply the interest rate times the balance, this gives me roughly what you will owe in a year. This is assuming you don't use the card for further purchases. Then you subtract 12 months times my minimum payment. This is where you will stand in one year if you are making only minimum payments. For example, let's say you owe $1,000 and the minimum payment is $20. Your interest rate is 20%. If you make your minimum payment every month, at the end of the year, you will owe approximately $1,000. Suppose you are still saving $250 per month on entertainment. If you take that savings and use it to pay your credit card payment. In five months you could pay off the balance. Not only are you out of debt, but you saved more than $100 in credit card interest. This shows how budgeting can bring you out of debt...

If you are carrying a balance on a number of cards, pay down the cards with the highest interest to start. If a credit card company offers a low interest introductory rate for transferring balances, you can consolidate some of your higher interest cards onto this new lower-interest card. Then you can pay it off. Please be careful because the introductory interest rate is often very different from the true rate on the card. The introductory rate is lower and after a limited period of time the rate goes up. It is therefore important to pay down the debt as well transfer it.

Other debt is important to pay off as well. Remember the aunt who leant you money when your car was broken down on the side of the road? Even though she is nice enough to charge no interest, it's important to use this same formula in paying her off. Assuming she leant you $360 to get your car repaired, it could be difficult to pay her off in one lump sum. However, $30 per month would take care of this debt in one year. You will probably feel a little less guilty when you see this aunt on the holidays. She may be more likely to help you in the future. You also will not have the stress of worrying about all the money you owe her. This frees you to receive more abundance because you have shown that you take care of debt and money responsibly. Once you have paid off the high interest debts, this opens the door to reducing other debts. There is a sweet liberation in paying things off that you owe, whether it is to a business or a personal loan.

Most people don't realize that by the time you've paid off a 30 year loan, you have paid off twice the amount you owed. If you make one extra payment each year on a 30 yr mortgage, it takes a 30 year mortgage and turns it into a 23 year mortgage. Not only do you pay your house off sooner, but you pay less interest. Similarly, if you pay off your car or any other debt sooner, you often pay less in interest. The interest rate does not have to be high to result in having less money in your pocket. For example, if you owe $100,000 on your home with a 6% loan, you end up paying back $200,000 in a 30 yr mortgage. If you made one extra payment per month, you would pay back approximately $180,000, which is a savings of $20,000 or 10%. If you don't have to spend $20,000, you can put it in the bank. Some people, before they retire, continue to put their mortgage payment in a savings account after the mortgage is completely paid. Since they were accustomed to paying that much every month before, it is easy to fit savings into their budget. It makes saving more painless.

Some people borrow against their houses to pay debt. If they don't eliminate the spending habits that led to their being in debt, then the plan doesn't make much sense. You risk losing one of your most valuable assets to pay off debt. You also have a higher mortgage loan amount and a longer time before you own your house outright. This can increase the interest rate on your loan as well. Sometimes the refinancing can delay paying your house by many years. If you can't pay your new higher mortgage payment, you may wind up with a short sale or foreclosure. Such events go against your credit, making it harder to buy or rent another house. It doesn't make much sense to refinance your house with a 30 year mortgage; say to buy a new car, since you still have 30 years worth of payments. This amounts to a total of 40 years of mortgage, 30 years of which are at a higher rate. This does not even include loan closing costs which can be thousands of dollars.

This brings us to impulse spending. Let's stick with the car example. If I have $10,000 for a down payment of a car that costs $30,000 or $40,000, instead I could buy a car that costs $10,000 outright. That way I have no monthly payment in case something comes up. I have no interest payment, so a $10,000 car is only costs $10,000 plus tax. I did not have to get more comprehensive insurance during the loan, which costs more. I didn't raise my mortgage payment for the next 30 years to get my car either. Because I bought a less expensive car, I pay less in car insurance and registration fees. I might not feel as proud driving cheaper older car, but I can feel more secure financially because what I save goes into the reservoir.

People impulsively spend on many smaller purchases as well. If you think about your closet, how many items have you never worn, or only worn a few times? These were once impulse buys. When Apple announces the new iPod or your cellular phone dealer promotes a new phone that takes videos, phone calls, emails, and text messages, do you buy it right away? How many times have you changed any product because they came out with something newer or better? The last time you moved, did you throw out old decorative household items because you had just bought some new ones? Did you go through your vase cupboard and get rid of five vases because you had four more than you actually use? These were impulse buys. There is no shame in making such purchases. Today you can simply identify them so that you are aware of your purchases tomorrow. Purchasing a few less such items can save you more money.

Here are some suggestions for avoiding impulse spending:

- Sleep on your purchase decisions. Is the item still alluring when you see it the next day or week?
- Window shop without credit cards in your pockets ahead of time. If you still want that item the following weekend, try to save up for it ahead of time. If you're meant to have it, it will be there the next weekend. How many of you regret not buying a blouse or pair of pants from the store? How many of you DO regret a clothing purchase?

- Make a list of what you intend to buy and stick to the list. When going to a large warehouse store where they have the impulse items at the end of each aisle, look away. If it's not on the list, you don't need it. Make sure you tell your children on your new plan. This way you can avoid the "see it want it have it" syndrome that big and little people can get into. Try the list method once to see if it changes your shopping habits and grocery bill totals.
- When you shop, use your check book or cash instead of credit card. If I have $20 in my pocket and I want to buy $40 worth of goods, the choice is simple. This is way less abstract than a credit card, perhaps because the cash isn't in front of you, and you're not handling it. You'll be glad you did this when the credit card bill comes in.
- If you believe that you might be depressed, anxious or have another emotional problem that contributes to your compulsive spending, get some treatment from a licensed psychotherapist who understands compulsive spending and who can help you create a treatment plan that addresses both your spending and the underlying emotional problem.
- Attend Debtors Anonymous and see if it feels like a good fit for you. Having other people around you who understand what you're going through and who have also lived with the same problems can be not only comforting but inspiring and helpful.

I have learned over the years that it's not what I make; it's what I spend that makes a huge difference in the size and health of my reservoir. Here are some examples of the difference between keeping up with, or exceeding one's income, and living within one's means.

Couple number one are Jim and Jamie. Jim made $500 per hour as consultant yet still was in debt. They went for a vacation by putting it all on their credit card. Five years later they still owed for the trip and have just been paying the interest. They went to Hawaii and it cost them $500 per person to fly each way, plus $200/night at a hotel, plus $600 for incidentals. A one week trip cost them $3,000. They paid for the trip almost twice because of the interest on their credit card. This makes a total of $6,000 for one week in Hawaii!

Couple number two consists of Mark and Susan. They took a tent, went to a local camp ground, and spent a week swimming, fishing and hiking. The cost was $400 out of pocket. Five years later they went to Hawaii, but bought everything out of pocket. They didn't spend ahead of their money and shopped for discounts for flight, lodging and accommodations. Their vacation cost 70% of the other couple's trip. They saved 100% by paying cash and not paying interest on their credit cards for five years. They saved a total of 140% compared to the cost of Jamie and Jim's trip. This made for a week in Hawaii for $2,100. This couple is they debt-free, *and* they went on two fun trips rather than one!

Sometimes one person in a marriage or family has a very different spending style than the other, and it creates significant problems. Money problems are one of the more frequent sources of conflict in couples. If you are not communicating well about how much and what you spend, it can lead to grave problems.

A man we'll call Pat has a demanding job that takes him away from home a lot. His wife Charlene is lonely and bored; she becomes resentful of his work and spends compulsively. Sometimes Charlene buys clothes without even trying them on, and then puts them into the closet with the price tag still on. Ralph gets mad at her and yells at her, which makes her angrier and more frustrated. She spends more to punish him for punishing her. The cycle continues until they are in debt and get divorced.

By contrast their friend George gets a less demanding and lucrative job that allows him to spend more time with his wife, Crystal. They have to be more careful about what they spend, but he is home more and they enjoy each other's company more frequently. George and Crystal argue very seldom about money and argue less in general. They set aside a certain amount of "free spending money" per month that they can each spend without consulting each other. However they each respect their commitment to each other (and themselves) not to exceed the agreed-upon amount. They discuss larger purchases ahead of time so they're in agreement and there are no surprise big credit card bills. They talk about problems they have openly and respectfully. When they are upset they deal with it as its happening rather than build up resentment. They try to come to a mutually agreeable solution to their problems. George and Crystal stay happily married and avoid incurring debt.

Writing Exercise: How You and Your Partner Handle Money

1. How are you similar to your partner or spouse in spending styles/habits?

_____

_____

2. How are you different from him or her in spending habits and styles?

_____

_____

3. How do you resolve these differences?

_____

_____

4. Is money a source of enjoyment or conflict in your relationship?

___

___

5. What can you do to get on the same page with your partner about money?

___

___

6. If you are single, how can you avoid conflicts about money with future romantic partners?

___

Investment

When you have established a savings program and are no longer keeping up with or exceeding your income with your purchases, you must then decide what to do with our money. A simple way to save is to get some of that money into a savings account that earns interest rather than just a checking account. When you choose where to put your savings, check the local institutions (banks, credit unions) for insured accounts that pay the best interest. You will not build your retirement nest egg on the small interests currently paid, but at least you will make something. There are some interest-bearing checking accounts available and often they require a minimum balance for that interest. Another simple way to save and invest is using an IRA account, which is for retirement. This takes money out of your check without taxing it. If you use a Roth IRA, you're not taxed when you put the money in or when you take that money out during retirement. This is a way of lowering your tax burden as well as saving for your future.

Certificates of deposit often earn greater interest than a savings account, but they make your money unavailable for a period of time. If you withdraw the money before the maturity date you risk losing any earnings by losing them to penalties.

Once you have achieved enough savings, the next step is investing. There are many choices for investment including money market accounts, stock market, real estate, etc. At this point, it's probably good to invest in seeing a financial planner who can help guide you in making the correct choices for your situation. Please be aware of what financial interests or products the advisor personally profits from. For instance does the advisor push some investment more than others? If so why? It can be a good rule of thumb to seek financial advice from someone with whom you are not investing. Also, shop around for an advisor before following any one person's advice. Have a standard list of questions you ask them, including what amount of fees he or she makes per year on your investment. If you have reached this point in your journey, congratulations! You can now make money from your existing money.

You don't have to work for the dollars your money makes. Make sure you read the fine print on any investment you want to pursue. Know about it, read about it, and think about it. so many people have lost a lot of money by entrusting their money to someone who told them what they wanted to hear, but not what they needed to know. If it seems too good to be true, then it most likely is. No one can or should look after your money like you do. The same is true of your health, relationships, and other areas of abundance. There is freedom and dignity, but also responsibility, in managing one's own life well. Being cautious and informed is a necessary brick in the foundation of good management.

It's also important to be careful how you discuss your new abundance. It might be prudent to be selective about which friends and family you tell, to avoid awkward situations involving envy and unpaid loans. This way, your money has a better chance of staying in your pocket. Please remember that you don't have to raise your expenses to match your income. This is how lotto winners go bankrupt. You can take satisfaction in knowing that your financial reservoir is continuing to fill, and you are prepared for any droughts. A final note here: it is good to have six months' worth of income in the bank that is accessible in case of illness, injury, or economic downturn. To figure how much money that is, you simply multiply one month's expenses in your budget by six.

A few basic ideas to avoid are: jumping into investments on impulse; believing the hype without investigating thoroughly; and investing in "collectible items." Many ads in magazines promise that you will be getting a collector's item with a certificate of authenticity. Before you invest in such an item as an investment, find out what the resale amount would be. For example, my father bought rare coins and stamps for me as an investment. I don't know if he considered the resale value or whether he just liked learning about the history behind the stamps and coins. I am sure he did some research, but who knows if he paid retail prices for something that will most likely be sold for wholesale prices? I would have to do even more research to discover whether his initial investment would pay off now. This is something to consider when purchasing "collectibles" – what resale value will the items have in the future? is it worth the initial cost of the item?

Here's another example of potential investment mistakes to avoid. Judy collected beanie babies as an investment and paid top dollar for the limited edition beanie babies because she believed they would be worth more money. She ended up with 40 beanie babies that cost an average of $18, or $720 total. Her friend Anita had trouble believing that beanie babies would gain value. Every time she had inkling to follow Judy's example, instead she put $18 in the bank. Twenty years later, Anita visited Judy and noticed that Judy's whole dining room table was covered with beanie babies. Judy was trying to raise money and offered Anita all of the beanie babies for $100. Anita bought two for $5 went home and put $13 in the bank. Anita saved $715 and earned interest on the money while Judy spent $720 and made a profit of $5.

Curb your enthusiasm… for spending.

As we saw above for some people, the line between investment and compulsive spending can be somewhat blurry. They "invest" in a variety of things, like cars, old radios, and any number of collections and things that have value to them but perhaps not other people. An investment is something you spend money on to make money. Sometimes folks forget that when they collect things. They might use the term investing to rationalize or justify collecting, or even hoarding. Compulsive spending is spending that costs you more than just the money to buy the items. It also has life damaging consequences, and it feels uncontrollable. For example, one might risk job loss by shopping online at work, or relationship loss because one spending is hurts other people. While it has not yet been classified by the mental health field as a mental disorder, some psychotherapists and psychiatrists are beginning to treat it as though it were a mental disorder[5]. While more research needs to be conducted to determine its causes and possible treatments, some researchers have found facts about it already. For example, at one clinic for impulse control disorders in UCLA, 40-50% of the people treated there for compulsive spending have another emotional problem along with it, such as depression, substance abuse, or anxiety disorders.[6]

A recent article in *Psychology Today* explained that there are differences in the way men and women spend compulsively. Male compulsive spenders tend to buy tools, cars, and books. They may get a competitive rush from obtaining the best deal on something. Women are more likely to buy shoes, clothes, and jewelry. Some studies suggest that there are just as many male compulsive

---

[5] Kuzma, J. and Black, D. Compulsive shopping: When spending begins to consume the consumer. *Journal of Family Practice, 5* (7), July 2006.
[6] Http://findmeacure.com/2008/07/28/compulsive-shopping-is-it-a-disorder/

spenders as women. However women tend to seek help for it more often, perhaps because it is more accepted for women to shop as a hobby.

The same article[7] classifies three types of over-spenders: emotional; bipolar; and obsessive. Each type has its own patterns of over spending. Emotional shopaholics spend money to change emotional states, but they notice that the change in mood is fleeting and they only feel that good while they're spending. Sadness is one mood state that often prompts people to shop compulsively, but anxiety, emptiness, and the inability to tolerate delayed gratification can also contribute to urges to spend compulsively[8]. Once the thrill of the hunt is gone, so is their good mood. Obsessive shopaholics, on the other hand, buy several varieties or colors of the same item, and do so to ensure feeling safe. They buy out of a sense of perfectionism, trying to get the best item possible. This will make them feel that they've reached an ideal. Both these types often regret their spending afterwards. By contrast people with Bipolar disorder do not often regret or feel remorse for over spending. For them compulsive spending is one of many symptoms of impaired judgment and reckless behavior. Bipolar shopaholics tend to spend beyond their means. They are often in temporary denial about what they can afford. Such shopaholics may think the money will magically appear to support their expenses. They may not stop once they've realized that they spent too much. All three types of compulsive spending are serious and need to be treated professionally.

How do you know if it's an addiction? While this book and workshop do not purport to treat or diagnose compulsive spending, here are some signs to watch out for. If you notice a pattern of these behaviors and traits, please speak to a licensed psychotherapist who specializes in compulsive behaviors:

- You feel shame about spending and keep it a secret from others in your life.

---

[7] Svoboda, Elizabeth. Shopaholic. *Psychology Today,* Sept./Oct. 2010, pp. 30-31.
[8] Bryner, Jeanna (2008). The truth about Shopaholics. Live Science. Http://www.livescience.com/health/080303-compulsive-shopper.html.

- You get a buzz from shopping that resembles a drug high or an altered state
- You lose or damage relationships because of your obsession with buying
- You put your livelihood (job, career) in danger with your spending habits (e.g., by stealing or using company time for shopping online)
- You spend so much on your shopping that you don't have money left over for essential items, or any other habits or activities
- You buy things out of a need to fill a sense of emptiness
- You spend money to avoid feeling negative emotions like anger, sadness or anxiety
- You buy things you don't need
- You spend money that you can't spare for what you purchase, or go into debt
- You consistently buy more than you intended, in greater amounts
- You become preoccupied with shopping even when you aren't currently shopping; you plan and obsess over it until you've made your purchase
- Your attempts to stop do not last for long and once you get going, you can't stop yourself.

There are also 12-step groups for compulsive spending, and if you call 211 in California, you can find a local meeting for Debtors Anonymous in your county if you are in California. They are an excellent way of helping yourself create support and structure for your recovery from compulsive spending. For more signs and information about this, please visit the Debtors Anonymous site: http://www.ncdaweb.org/12Signs.html

One way to begin working on compulsive spending is to honestly look at why you're doing it and try to find another way to be happy or satisfied. For example, you can practice gratitude for what you already have. When you think of what you need, take time to also think about what you already have. Take your mind from "I need this" to "I have that". It gives you pause, so you can create a different mental reality. Sometimes the anxiety about not having enough can be eased when you look in your closets or drawers at what you have already purchased. You are less focused on what you don't have than on what you do have. Once you have started addressing this leak in the dam (if it applies to you), you will notice that you have enough time, money and love to help you feel complete. Your life will also be more manageable and satisfying.

Pulling out the roots of compulsive spending…

Ingrained spending habits are often learned in childhood from modeling after (copying) our parents' spending habits. Some people try to do the opposite of what their parents did regarding money others find themselves doing the exact same behaviors. People can also, spend one way for a long time, then rebel. Often people self-correct to a set point that they learned growing up. How could you change that? Ask yourself, where will this item be five years from now? Many people don't consider what they will do with the items they buy. They also don't consider where the item will be stored. If they consider the cost and time in caring for and cleaning the item they might put it back on the store shelf. Another question is how many hours will it take to make the money back? How long did it take you to earn the money you spend on this item? Is it worth it? Consider whether you want to work that many hours again to replace that money you've spent.

How does this fit into your budget? Think about large bills you have to pay. Do you have money available after you've paid those large bills? Is the money left over enough to comfortably spend this money now? Do you have enough of a cushion in case something bad happens that costs money? What if your loved one becomes ill? Do you have enough money left over if the car breaks down or you break your leg? It might help it you tell yourself that you have less disposable income than you actually have. Keep yourself in touch with your funds by balancing your checkbook regularly so you know what you have. Being realistic and informed are two very helpful ways to avoid unnecessary stress over money. You have the power to take control of your spending by examining the root causes and realistic patterns. In the end it's all just stuff you are buying.

Do you really need all the stuff you have? Look in your closets, drawers, and storage spaces. Is there anything that you could do without comfortably? Do you have things in these spaces that you haven't seen or used in years? What good are they doing you? Think about what it would be like to need and have less? What feelings and thoughts arise as you consider this? Ponder the difference is between needing and wanting something. Most of us can agree that we need food, water, shelter, and air. Beyond that, how much do we truly need, and how much is convenient or pleasant to have? When was the last time you truly needed something you purchased? What was that item?

Writing exercise: What You Have, Who You Are

What is most precious in the world to you?

_____

_____

What if everything you owned were suddenly taken away? Who would you be? What would be your worth?

_____

_____

How would you feel about yourself?

_____

_____

What do you have that cannot be taken away from you?

_____

_____

So now you have the tools to keep money in your reservoir, you have debt paid down, and you may even have money making you money. Terrific! Keep up the good work! Now is the time to relax about money, provided that you keep up the good habits. I read in the *Los Angeles Times* Business section a money makeover column on a couple who actually under-spent! They had plenty of money to retire, but kept working at jobs about which they weren't that thrilled, and lived extremely frugally. They had enough but didn't enjoy it much. I knew another elderly couple that used 25 watt light bulbs and damaged their eyes because they didn't want to spend the extra electricity, while they had nearly $600,000 in the bank plus their home in a nice area. While such people are probably the exception to the rule of spending, they are vital teachers to avoid over-emphasizing the importance of spending and saving. There are some things on which you can use money that make good sense (at least to me). Some of these are: good health care; comfortable shoes; a healthy home in a safe neighborhood; a safe, reliable car; and a good education for you and/or your children.

Health is the most valuable asset you have. If you're doing an unhealthy job, it is probably a good idea to retrain for one that will not risk your health as much. You may also try to get promoted so that you can work less directly with harmful materials or in unhealthy buildings. With sedentary jobs, there is the risk of becoming unhealthy because your heart is not challenged enough and it's easier to gain weight. Offices also have candy and popcorn around every holiday season. If you're in a sedentary job, try to get up and move during the course of the day. Try to get fresh air as well. Use the stairs whenever possible instead of the elevator.

Living in a safer neighborhood is important as well in terms of safety and stress. It's better to have the fixer-upper house in a safe neighborhood than a fancier house in a more dangerous neighborhood. You can make a tougher neighborhood safer by participating in neighborhood watch programs, talking to your city council members about crime in your area, or simply anonymously calling the police when you see trouble. If you have children, you might want to choose the neighborhood where you live according to school quality and safety so that they are safe and well-educated. You also want to make sure that your home is free of toxic mold and other environmental hazards as well as dangerous pests.

Good shoes may seem silly to you. However, having seen the effects of bad shoes, I am a big fan of comfortable, well-made shoes. I knew a woman whose feet were actually deformed because she wore high heels that were too small for her. I know other people who have slipped and fallen because the soles of their shoes had no traction. The shoes you get at discount places are often poorly made, don't last, and often have to be replaced more often. This reduces the initial savings to zero. Invest in a few pairs of nice, well-made, comfortable shoes and your feet, and the rest of your body, will thank you later.

We've already discussed the value of a good education for you. It makes a difference in your earning capacity, your understanding of the world, and your quality of life. The same consideration should be extended to your children. When you decide to have children, please think about how you will clothe, feed, house and educate them. Where do you want them to grow up? How will that affect their quality of life? Will they be on their own for college? Will you want to educate them privately? As calculating as it sounds, these are real life concerns to consider before you conceive. What does it cost to raise a child? How will you provide for your child or children? How will you manage to keep your financial stress from seeping onto them? I see many people in therapy who felt like a burden to their over-stressed parents, who had many children. They expected the older ones to raise the younger ones, since the parents were so busy. Fortunately we're in an age when we can decide when to have kids and how many. Why not take advantage of this and plan for your children financially? It's not too late to start saving for their futures such as college.

The Next Generation....

As obvious as this may sound, teach your kids about savings and don't give them whatever they want so they'll like you. The more guidance you give them when they're young, the better prepared they will be to deal with the real world. Show them from an early age that you budget and plan for things you want to buy. Give them a little bit of money and explain to them how to save for their toys, music, TV, iPod, etc. They will take better care of an item they saved for versus one you bought and then replace when they break it.

I see many parents of teens who regret not having done this when they were younger. Often it's very hard to put the brakes on an adolescent who's used to getting his or her own way. Set a good example for them so they can see how to handle money responsibly. You and your children will benefit as a result. This doesn't mean that you hold over their heads every expense you have for them. They didn't ask to be born, so if you send them to violin lessons, please don't try to make them feel guilty or indebted to you for it. However, you can say to them (if they're not practicing very much or not seeming to enjoy it), "It seems like you are not very interested in this at this point. Should we talk about whether you want to continue with this activity?" You can also ask them to do extra chores to help pay for the cost of the activity. This is especially useful to motivate children if they are not participating in the activity to their full potential. Perhaps your child wants to do football but isn't exercising or practicing for his sport. Have him mop the floors or rake leaves for you once a week to help pay for it. Explain that you are willing to have them stop when you see that they are taking the practice seriously. That way they are more motivated to put their all into the activity. Worst case scenario, you have cleaner floors. Keep in mind that this can be taken too far, so try to have an honest discussion with the child first. See if they are other factors that keep him or her from full participation, like homework or a difficulty of some sort.

Another way to teach your children about the value of money is though allowance. Allowance is a way to give kids spending money that they earn. It helps them connect spending to earning. You can also have them do jobs beyond the usual chores (like keeping their rooms picked up). Give them a room besides their own to keep clean on a weekly basis. They do their chores to get their allowance; it's that simple. If they saved their allowance for what they want, they can have it. if they did not save, they can't have it. Chores should be assigned within reason for age and ability level. However, children don't learn to be self-sufficient without doing these things. If they don't do it well at first, give them gentle and constructive correction. However, if they are consistently careless in their efforts, you can pay what you think they earned; for example, if they put in 50% effort, pay them 50% of their allowance. They view any time away from what they enjoy as an imposition, so don't load them down with too many chores Try to be even-handed and calm about chore assignments. When they do well, tell them! You can give praise freely and liberally. It gives much more satisfaction to the budding laborer than money. Be generous with praise and judicious with financial rewards.

CHAPTER 4
MAKING OPPORTUNITIES HAPPEN

When the Law of Attraction became a popular New Age phenomenon, many people seemed to think that declaring what they wanted should be sufficient to achieve abundant wealth. Boy, were they disappointed when checks didn't start rolling in just because they thought they should. The Law of Attraction is not wrong. It is just part of the equation in creating abundant wealth. Beliefs *are* powerful. A clear vision of what you want will surely prepare you to receive it just as the Law of Attraction states. However you still need to get off the couch and take action to achieve your version of abundance. You don't lose weight by sitting around eating. You don't quit smoking by saying "I'll do than tomorrow." Change requires risk and stepping outside your comfort zone. It also means tolerating the new experiences and bumps in the road that ensue as you act on your own behalf. Any kind of lasting success is won through effort as well as inspiration. This brings us to the next topic of applying effort.

Network – whenever, wherever you are, with whomever you're speaking

A trip to the gas station, a store, or a friend's house can all be opportunities for networking. When my good friend was a teenager, he was blessed with such a chance meeting. He was on his way to his friend's house and took the elevator in the friend's apartment complex. While in the elevator, he struck up a conversation with one of the other passengers, who happened to work there. This way, he found out about a job in the apartment complex and applied for it. He started the conversation by asking the other fellow about himself, and found that the other guy (like most people) liked talking about himself. He expressed a sincere interest in the other person's life. This opened the passenger up to talking more freely. This is a good way to approach networking. This is opposed to the person who starts out by talking about himself. He shows no interest in you or lets you get a word in edgewise. Such a person is less likely to attract others, personally or professionally.

The opposite of networking is lying on the living room couch. Not many job opportunities ring your front door bell. Wherever you go during your day, treat people with kindness and respect. Everyone from the counter staff at Starbucks to the gas station clerk is happy to be treated with care and decency. You can ask them what it's like to work for their company. Do they get paid well? Are they happy? Are there any job openings? Especially in today's company, many jobs are filled before they are advertised. If they are not filled internally, they are filled by friends or family members who have found out about the job before the position is advertised. Similarly you can use social networking, like Facebook or MySpace to find out about jobs before they are filled. If you get a lead from there, you must act on it right away, because other people will see the lead as well. Don't forget to treat others with dignity, and always show gratitude and respect. A potential job or friend is potentially there wherever you go.

I know these are desperate times for many people. There is always a labor pick up spot in any community and many people are happy to pay cash for day laborers. If we can set our pride aside, we can go to a spot like that and at least get a day's work. You never know if the person who hires you that day might know of another job opportunity. I realize that such a position is not anybody's dream, but it's a way to make money and meet people. This assumes that the people who hire you see you as a person. I have talked with people who insisted on waiting for middle management positions but wound up taking fast food jobs. It beats losing one's home to foreclosure, in my opinion. At chain restaurants, the workers used to be teenagers. Now many older people work there. It can fill the gap in income until their next desired opportunity arises. Once again, you will be exposed to more people than if you're sitting at home. You can network for jobs, friends, and connections this way.

I find that if you submit a resume online to a prospective employer one day, it's best to go meet the people in person the next day. At least follow up with a phone call. This is another chance to form a relationship with people, even if it's "just" the receptionist. Consider that the receptionist is the gatekeeper for the company; he or she probably knows a little about the company. The receptionist handles mail, email, phone calls, and other forms of communication for some important people. If you can stand out as someone who treats him or her well, your efforts at communication might make it through the competitive influx of people that the company deals with daily. Learn about them as people and give your interactions a personal touch, like" How is little Jenny?" if they have a daughter. Don't be afraid to make notes after meetings and phone calls, to remember such details about them as a person. People are often flattered and appreciate this effort. However, you don't have to restrict this sort of "get to know you" strategy to the people in the companies where you'd like to work. You can also do this with whomever you meet.

The more people you meet, the more chances you have to communicate about things that are important to you. However, you have to put yourself out there and take the chance of being rejected. Some people prefer the emotionally safety of staying at home and feeling bad for themselves. That seems better than going out and trying for a job, or even going to the library. The daily paper is available at the library for free; it lists job opportunities. The librarian and clerks at the library know about employment opportunities working there. By developing a relationship with them, or a grocery store clerk, or any one of many people with whom you come into contact during the week, you can build relationships. These can become opportunities for work or friendship. If they know you, and they know you're looking for work, they will be more likely to think of you when something comes up. They might tell you about a job or mention you to their employer. If you can't get out of the house, or out of bed, for more days than not, you might not be depressed or anxious. It is important to get treatment for these conditions so that you can feel better. Then you can have the life that you want and deserve. By treating the root causes, you will be able to get out of the house and employ these networking ideas.

People often advertise on the internet and have web pages, submit resumes online, etc. That is a valuable way to get your name out there. Yet there are still some people like me who enjoy putting a face to a name, shaking a hand and looking into the eyes of another human being. I don't often refer to other psychotherapists whom I have not personally met. I want to make sure that if I can't help a potential client, they will wind up with someone I know, like, and trust. In looking for a job via the internet, it is important to try to make yourself stand out as well. After you have submitted your application online, try to find a way to contact the company offline. I find that in person is the best, but if that is not an option, a phone call can help. This way you can separate yourself from their many other choices employers have.

Another approach is to talk to people at other companies. Talk to people who are in the position you'd like to be in, ask them how they got where they are and see if they have any advice or ideas. Take them out to lunch or coffee, ask them about their successes (who doesn't like to boast a bit), and explore with them what they like and dislike about their jobs. Unless it was sheer nepotism (they were in the same family as their boss), there is something that you can learn and apply for your own situation. For example, if you are a bank teller and want to be a personal banker, you can take out a personal banker at another bank (so the personal banker at your bank doesn't feel threatened). When I was graduating from college, they called this "informational interviewing." Don't be afraid to be part of your alumni association and go to job fairs at local colleges. Keep in touch with employers from old businesses where you've worked (assuming the work relationship ended amicably). Don't call them constantly, but occasionally calls or emails won't hurt. Don't be afraid to compliment the person with whom you are speaking by mentioning the things you admire about him or her. At best you wind up with a job; at worst, you just might make a friend.

Formal ways to network include groups like Business Networkers International, your local Chambers of Commerce, Rotary Clubs, Lions Clubs, etc. I like to call other therapists and invite them to coffee or lunch. Some enterprising therapists have also hosted open houses or networking meetings in their offices. You can get creative about how to reach out and meet new people, or you can go the traditional routes and use existing venues like business networking clubs. However, you can also think outside the box. Are there any hobbies you enjoy that others enjoy too? Talk to your fellow quilters, horticulturalists, anglers, and see how their businesses are going. Remember that this is a personal relationship as well as a business opportunity. Remember to treat them with dignity, respect, and consideration. Don't just talk about work, and remember to treat the person first as a person, second as a business contact.

Writing Exercise: Networking
1. What networking have you done that has improved your business?

_____

_____

2. What people are you going to see next week with whom you can apply a new networking strategy?

_____

_____

3. What kind of networking works for you in job hunting/business building and what has not worked?

_____

_____

4. For the ways that have worked, what did you do to make these efforts successful?

_____

_____

5. For the methods that haven't worked, what went wrong? What was your part in the method not succeeding? (Try to objective and *not* self-punitive!)

_____

_____

Lead with, "What can I do for you?" (No one likes a Taker)

After you have established some personal rapport with a person, then lead with what you can do for the other person's business/interests. This is the idea behind Business Networking International.One of their slogans is that "givers get," meaning that giving referrals and assistance to others begets receiving referrals. If people sense that you are just trying to use them or get something from them, they are usually turned off. There is a fine balance between assertively getting what you want, and being pushy or selfish. Help people feel that you are interested in them more than their job connections. They can often tell if you don't respect and or value them as humans. I often ask people about their lives, such as whether they are married, have children, or what they do recreationally. A show of interest can bring out a story from the person's recent family life. This also opens a personal door for me. Then I can go on to asking them how they like their jobs or what interested them in the field where they work. This could lead to a question about whether their company is hiring, or whether they have occasion to refer to your kind of business. If this is done with people lined up behind me in a store, it might not all be accomplished in one visit. When I go to that store again, I could look for my favorite checker and continue to build the relationship. Long after you find a job or build your client base, you will still have people you know and enjoy talking to around your community.

When you refer people to a business that you especially like, call the business to let them know. You can also remind them that you are open for referrals too. Don't count on the person you referred to the other business to mention you by name. Call them or write them and let them know that you have referred that person. This encourages the other business person to think of ways to return the favor. It also increases the good will you share with that business person. If that person does not refer people back to you, perhaps an in-person meeting would help you understand what's going on. Alternately, you could find a different referral source that reciprocates more.

You also want to "toot your own horn," so to speak. Let others know when you've succeeded or keep a file of customer compliments, including the name, date and time of the new accounts or new customers you bring in (if you're employed by someone else). The same holds true when you are looking to find a job; don't be afraid to mention your qualifications as well as the fact that you're "between jobs." If you are unemployed, it makes you seem more desirable because you're more confident and upbeat, since you are describing your successes as well as your current situation. If you already have a job, presenting your victories and successes, may not guarantee an immediate raise or promotion, but should pay off in the future.

If you're self-employed, review your successes to yourself for encouragement. Let others know about your achievements in a way that doesn't sound like bragging. Your best marketing tool is client satisfaction. Encourage referrals by offering a slight discount to your satisfied clients who refer to you. This is assuming that your job legally or ethically allows such a practice. Of course, advertising is the ultimate tooting of one's own horn. You can also write articles for the local paper that let your community know about your business, or volunteer to speak on topics related to your business in the community. Some people write newsletters and send them to their business contacts to keep in touch with people they've met at networking meetings. The idea is to communicate about your business in a periodic and pleasant way. The opposite of this are the companies that send you newsletters much more often than you'd like. The letter should not be more boastful than you'd like to hear. The newsletter, like the speech, should be informational, and not just an advertisement for you or your company. For example, if I am a fruit salesman, I could talk about how to pick the right kind of produce and then mention that I sell good produce at the end.

You can use marketing in your down time as a way to keep the pipeline of customers coming to your business when things get slow. I've seen with my practice that summer is a slow period of time for business, because of vacations and the heat. I can't change summer into a busier season but the marketing I do then pays off threefold in the winter and early spring. Kids go back to school and exhibit behavior issues, resulting in referrals for play therapy. Adults go see their families for the holidays and it brings up past family of origin issues, leading to referrals for trauma therapy. The seeds sown in summer come to fruition later on. This is a way of taking spare time and turning it into a money maker.

When times get slow or the job gets tough, it's time to work a little harder to bring in the work. In these slow economic times, when employers consider layoffs, you want to be remembered as the worker who applies himself or herself. You don't want to be the employee who texts at work or has an entitled attitude. It helps to envision what your potential customer or employer would see as an optimal service provider. If your supervisor or company take you for granted or ignores your efforts, you can continue to work well so that you can obtain a good reference from your current boss. That way you can get a better job elsewhere with the aid of that reference.

I knew a man who worked as a front office staff person for two months. Joel was then approached by his boss who wanted her to train his daughter for Joel's position. Furthermore, the boss wanted to demote Joel to working under his daughter for less money. At this point, Joel was furious (and probably with good reason!). He had two choices: agree to fulfill his demands in exchange for a good letter of reference, or quit and tell the boss off. The latter choice would turn his boss into a negative reference-giver. Unfortunately, Joel chose the latter option and became under-employed. There's no guarantee that his boss would have fulfilled his end of the promise. However, there was a possibility that the boss would come through for Joel and find someone else to work for his business. Joel felt bitter about working for that industry and felt that all bosses there would be equally as exploitive as this boss. What other options could he have employed?

Still not sure about getting off the couch?

Here are some other ideas for making opportunities happen:

- Make yourself available to the community (see and be seen by others)
- When you go out in public, try to look presentable so you will leave a decent first impression
- Volunteer at a local social service agency or organization, or even walk the dogs at the pound – just get out and be friendly, approachable and meet people!
- Hand out business cards or flyers at local shopping centers
- Research companies you'd like to work for. Try to get an internship there, to learn "from the ground up"
- When you say, "I work at X Company", try to say it with as much pride as you can muster. It may not be your dream job, but if you insult your employer around people you meet, it can be a turn-off. Imagine how that sounds to the other person. Might they wonder, "If that's how they talk about their current boss, what would they say about working for my company?" Be proud if you have *any* job in this economy! That's no mean feat anymore!
- Cold call if you're in business for yourself. Get used to the idea that some people might not want what you have, but some might. Follow up and see if they need anymore business cards or brochures.
- Respect your boundaries and others'. If they're not interested, that's ok! Don't be so aggressive that people dodge you at cocktail parties. I knew a real estate agent who was so pushy about trying to get referrals (yet also lazy at her job), that I made it a point NOT to refer her to anyone.
- Be the employee you would want to have if you were a manager or business owner. Don't text or make personal calls on the job, don't have a poor attitude when asked to do something, and don't argue with your boss about job duties.

- If you need to learn how to be a suave business person, learn from the best – try to find a mentor who is good at sales and has interpersonal finesse.

At first doing these things might feel awkward and you might feel shy. One powerful motivator is being hungry. If I'm hungry, I want to be fed. In order to eat, I have to work. So I make a few cold calls and try to generate business or I go out to meet a new therapist or doctor. If I'm too busy in my practice to keep up with it, I can slow down on the cold calls. But I don't stop altogether, because I want to keep a steady stream of referral sources and referrals coming to me. I used to be shy (and I still am an introvert), but I am also the main breadwinner for the family. I put aside my personal feelings about rejection, and occasional laziness. I do what it takes to put a roof over our heads and food on the table. This brings us to the issue of commitment.

Over-commitment vs. Under-commitment

As you market yourself to potential employers or referral sources (or clients), make sure you can fulfill the promises and proclamations you make about yourself or your skills. Be willing to back these up in full, or you could get a bad reputation.

We recently went to a furniture store that said they would "meet or beat any price". However, when we showed them an ad with a competitor's price for the same item, they acted resentfully for matching the competitor's price. Needless to say, we're not rushing to buy any more furniture from that place. Not only did they lie in their ad, they also acted unprofessionally and that manager lost his company business with this bad attitude.

That is an example of under-commitment. Under committed people text and make personal calls while at work. They may set a goal of making twelve cold calls in a week and only complete two. They talk about how they will accomplish lofty goals but do not put any action in that direction. Under commitment can be seen in minimal or disorganized action as well. One might plan to market their business or apply for new jobs and not follow through. Needless to say, no one will meet new customers or find a job if they sit around, watching TV.

It's important to evaluate whether your goals are realistic. Do you have the skills, knowledge, and internal and external resources to reach that goal? First you identify a deficit in one of these areas. Then you try to either get what you need to correct the deficit or adjust your goal to account for your current circumstances. Commitment helps you do things you know you need to do, even though you might not like doing them.

Do you know what a cold call is? Have you ever made one? A cold call is a call to someone you do not know trying to get new business or a job. If you're in sales, that's often an integral part of your job every day. Do you like making them? Not everyone does, but it's a central technique of sales and marketing. While everyone likes the results, not many people like the process of actually doing it. Committed people set a goal of working a certain number of cold calls and follow through, even when it's boring or uncomfortable. Cold calls to employers for jobs work as well. They can be done on the phone or in person.

Over-committed people, by contrast, often work so hard they don't see their own loved ones or family. They may bring out their business card when introducing themselves before establishing a need for such action. This is premature before they establish a relationship with the person. They are so eager to make business contacts that they treat people as means to an end. In other words, people are just objects or potential customers to them. They skip holidays to work or make new business contacts. Some may call them workaholics.

Anyone who has ever watched "Gene Simmons Family Jewels" can see an example of a classic workaholic. He is financially wealthy, yes. But would you want to be his romantic partner or be part of his family on vacation? He seems to use all his time to market and make money, and very little spending quality time with his friends and family. Would you want to be so obsessed with one type of abundance that other areas of your life suffer? How much is enough, already?

Writing Exercise: Over-Commitment and Under-Commitment

1. How much wealth is enough for you? At what point can you relax and take some time off work?

_____

_____

2. Where would you put yourself on this continuum, and why? Make a mark where you think you are.

|--|--|
Under-committed　　　　　　　　　　Healthy　　　　　　　　　　Over-committed

3. Do you know of someone who works so much they can't unwind or be/have fun? What can you learn from them?

_____

_____

4. Do you know a person who dreams big but does not put their plans into action? What do you think and feel about them? What can you learn from them?

_____

_____

It's important to find a good balance between work and play. I'm not suggesting that you I just let everything go and become a beach bum. Hard, honest work should be rewarded, but so should being human and not allowing greed or money-lust dominate one's life. British psychologist Adrian Furnham, PhD[9] points out that money can be used to meet so many different emotional needs, such as power, love, affection, freedom, and self worth. I suggest that we re-evaluate the role it plays in our lives, so that it remains a means of exchange for goods and services that we need. We can still get our emotional needs met, but perhaps we can find different ways to get those needs met. It seems that when money becomes central to a person's life, it can block out other important aspects of our existence. We can use money to help ourselves and others, or we can use it to manipulate, exploit, or deceive others. The choice is ours, but we don't realize that it's a choice until we examine our thoughts and feelings about money. We have been doing that in this book. As we examine our values, we can make a conscious decision to achieve harmony in the different areas of our lives.

One way to achieve balance is to make our goals realistic. Our goals need to be high enough to stimulate us to action and intrigue us so we follow through. If the goals are so high that they're daunting and intimidating, we might feel ashamed when we don't reach them. This may sap our motivation and energy, especially if we are unkind with ourselves when we don't make the mark. If we set our goals too low, we don't give ourselves credit that we can achieve greatness and have the lives we want. It's important to set your goals at a reasonable level.

If you tend to be under committed here are some tips. When you need a break from your job, make it a time-limited thing. Give yourself a half hour to do whatever you want, but don't get lost in your diversion. Some things, like the internet, can suck you in and waste much more time than you intended. After you

---

[9] Psychology of Money, http://ebookbrowse.com/presentation-adrian-furnham-pdf-d39062025

have spent a half an hour of video games, TV or the internet in one day, cut back to 20 minutes a day. That frees up 1 ½ hrs per week that could be spent on creating wealth. Try to save your distractions for after work. It's just like when you were a kid and had homework. When you did the homework early, it was easier to have guilt-free fun.

If you're overcommitted, you can use this book and workshop as a tool to explore that tendency. Many perfectionists are overcommitted and have a penchant for all or nothing thinking. If they don't perform exactly to their high expectations, they feel like utter failures. It's important to see the shades of gray between failure and success. Acknowledge your small successes as they are achieved on the journey toward your goals. This can help you feel less stress, anxiety, and poor self esteem. When you are working so hard that you ignore other important aspects of your life (like health or family), you may be working compulsively. This pattern may be helping you escape an unresolved issue from the past. Self exploration, self help groups like workaholics anonymous and psychotherapy can help you. They can bring you to the root of the problem and give you tools to have a more harmonious and satisfying life.

Success is about making a reasonable commitment to performance. Whether you're self-employed or working for someone else, success isn't a matter of getting away with working at least as you can. Instead it's about giving your best effort on a regular basis. When you have harmony in your life, you will be able to perform better because you won't be under-stimulated. Nor will you be burned out from burning the candle at both ends. Finding the right mixture of rest and work for you will take time. Nonetheless, it's worth exploring and working towards a happy medium. If you can master this, your abundant wealth will feel more worthwhile and enjoyable to you.

Givers Get… The Sequel

Every success I have had in my life has depended on help, or cooperation from, others. At times even the resistance from other people has spurred me on to succeed. Being told I can't do something sometimes makes me rebellious. I become more independent and fiercely committed to my goal at those times. I cannot succeed alone. I need help from others to make my dreams come true. The moment I forget this is the moment that I risk losing what I have. Otherwise, I can become greedy and self-delusional, thinking that I did it all by myself. I believe that it's important to acknowledge the people who helped us and treat them with the gratitude and respect they deserve.

Give back to people who have helped you in whatever way you can. If they have helped you get a job, you can make them a meal or write them a thank you card. If they have referred to your business, give them something extra that will let them know you appreciate their efforts. We all like to be appreciated and acknowledged! When people refer clients to me, I send them a $10 gift card for the local coffee store. It lets them know I appreciate their confidence and kindness in referring to me. Other times I bring them cookies or brownies. It may sound corny, but how many doctors or therapists get this sort of treatment? Probably not enough of them are treated with appreciation. When I network with other therapists or health professionals, I ask them what their areas of specialization are and what kind of referrals they want. That way if I have a potential client with that problem and I cannot help them myself, I can send them to that therapist. I also tell them what type of referrals I would like. This is all a way to be abundant and let my humanity come through. I try to be the kind of person with whom others would like to do business. By doing so, I also like myself better for being humble, and kind to others.

Writing Exercise: Who Are Your Helpers?

1. Write a list of people who have helped you get to where you are today. Was it your parents, who made you do your homework and eat your broccoli? A special teacher who believed in you? A boss who took a chance on you? Supportive coworkers? Who has been instrumental in your climb to success so far?

_____

_____

2. What are some ways that you have already thanked them?

_____

_____

3. What are some ways you can let them know that you appreciate what they've done? What would you want done for you if the roles were reversed?

_____

_____

4. Are there people whom you have helped in the past? How do you feel about this? What kind of feeling do you get from helping him/her?

_____

_____

CHAPTER 5

SHARING AND ENJOYING YOUR WEALTH

At some point, you will amass enough wealth for you and your family to live comfortably. You might even be considered rich. What will you do with the rest? Save it for a rainy day? That's not a bad plan. I'd like you to expand your vision to think about people who don't have anything at all. Believe it or not, sometimes giving to others creates a kind of abundance that money can't buy. It's spiritual wealth that tells you that you have done the right thing for someone else. Whether it's a friend who needs your help or a total stranger, the feeling you get from giving can be just as rewarding as having a new car.

Charity is not just about tax write-offs! There are people and creatures (animals, fish, plankton… you get the idea) in this world that have less than we do. We can be a blessing to those creatures in whatever way we feel comfortable. In this section we will talk about what to do once you feel comfortable that you've saved enough for yourself and your loved ones. How can you enjoy it within reasonable bounds? How do you know what reasonable bounds are? Each person defines this to some extent for themselves. These are the guidelines that make sense to me.

One thing I always feared about having money was that it would make me a snob, or a conceited jerk. That's what I *used to* believe about people with money. After looking at my beliefs, however, I realized that not all rich people are like that. There are conceited jerks in every corner of society, not just among people with money. I decided that I was not being helped by this belief. However, like I said before, I like to eat. I still have to keep things in perspective. I don't want to be a workaholic or a snobby, conceited jerk. And I don't want to burn out.

All work and no play make me a pain in the rear to be around. I become irritable, stressed, short-tempered, depressed, anxious, overwhelmed, distracted, and physically unhealthy. So I take my weekends off (aside from writing this book, which I actually consider fun) and swim, socialize, and try to enjoy myself. The rest of the time I work hard. I don't want to be a pain to be around, for others or myself. At a certain point, I need to say, "Yes, Lisa, you did well. You worked, you earned, and you helped people, now rest!" This allows me to go to the museum, read the Sunday paper, paint, draw, etc. If I didn't do that, I'd be obsessed with making money. That would be unhealthy and out of harmony with the rest of my life. While, I'm not super-wealthy (or even wealthy by some people's standards) I am pretty content.

Money can be a source of security. Knowing that bills are paid, a roof is over my head, and having a job that I love gives me security. It allows me to have relatively worry-free down time. After all, what good is wealth you never get to have fun?

What do you do with your down time? (If you're asking what down time is, that's a bad sign!) What do you do to relax?

I am not religious, but I do believe in a creative force in the universe that provides strength and support for all of us. Yes, I have worked hard and made sacrifices to get where I am. However, without other people (who I know and don't know), I could not have been successful as I am today. I want for everyone to have good health, happiness, and prosperity. Even if I can give food to someone who has nothing or less than me, I feel better. What good is my wealth if I don't give back to the community? I define the community loosely, as I think we are all inter-connected on this planet. In a way we're all brothers and sisters. The community can be your neighborhood, city, state, country, or the world at large. There are so many people who can use my help, or your help. Is there a cause that speaks to your heart, about which you feel passionately? What can you do to help that cause? For me it's people with HIV and AIDS, because they have faced so much discrimination and hatred.

What is your cause? Who will be the beneficiaries of some of your resources?

_____

_____

Notwithstanding, I hope that you remember to keep your giving in perspective and balance as well. Don't give so much to others that you are living in poverty/debt yourself. This may sound obvious to you, but there are some people who feel compelled to give even at their own peril or risk. One nice elderly lady I know had a big house up in San Francisco. She had a roommate, Sam, who was divorced and had a child. The lady needed to move out of the area to be closer to her son, and offered to sell the house to Sam for what she paid for it. The home had appreciated during the real estate boom while she owned it. She wanted Sam to have a nice home for his child. He took her up on that offer but instead of keeping it for himself, he bought it with an investor friend of his and flipped it for profit. This broke the lady's heart. Not only had Sam lied to her about the purpose of his purchase, but she also missed out on the $100,000 she could have made from the profit had she simply sold it to the highest, best offer. Her charity was exploited, and so she didn't feel fulfilled by her giving.

Many elderly people also get exploited by charities that send relentless mail for various causes. Some folks may lack the charity to remember which charities they sent money to. They might also give to false organizations that are not true charities. Once your name is on one charity's mailing list as a donor, some charities sell your name and address to other charitable organizations. Check out the charity to which you want to give, and make sure that it is a legitimate non-profit organization that uses the funds for the purposes stated. See how much of the collected funds go to the administration of the organization, and how much go to the actual cause. Like any expenditure, think carefully about it and make sure the money you give will go to a worthy cause. That way you will not feel used and deceived. Also, choose one or two causes that you will support and put a cap on how much you will donate those causes. That way you won't get caught up in a giving frenzy that leaves you broke or in danger of being broke.

If you feel unsafe sharing your dollars and cents, share your time with others. For example, you could volunteer at an organization or club you believe in, spend some time babysitting for the neighbors, rake up your friend's leaves, help a housebound neighbor take their trash cans in, etc. This also increases a sense of spiritual abundance, giving you sense of greater purpose while also deepening your connection to other people and creatures. You say you don't feel comfortable with people? Try walking dogs or taking care of cats at the local animal shelter No, you don't have to take them all home to take care of them! Another idea is to take care of wounded animals at a wildlife refuge. Clear up trash from the street or the beaches. Write letters for Amnesty International. There are many ways to share your abundance with others in the world.

Enjoy the ebb and flow of wealth in your life and again… RELAX.

Writing Exercise:

1. What are some of the things you've wanted to do with your wealth?

___

___

2. How do you plan to enjoy the fruit of your labors? Take a vacation? Buy something you've always wanted?

___

___

3. How do you feel about sharing your wealth with others? What do you feel when you contemplate this?

___

___

4. Are there some ways that you already help others in your community? How do you feel about that? Is it enough, in your opinion? Or do you want to do more?

___

___

CHAPTER 6

CREATING AN ACTION PLAN TO CREATE MORE ABUNDANT WEALTH IN YOUR LIFE

This is your chance to think creatively about how you will generate abundant wealth in your life. Try to be specific and detailed about it. Don't edit or second guess yourself. Throw a bunch of ideas onto the paper at first. Then later pick the idea you like best. It's fun to do this with other people to see the synergy that happens when you and those around you get excited. The group can share many ideas. Try to be gentle with yourself and others and don't shoot down people's dreams with negative comments. Have fun with this!

A.   What is your idea that will create more abundance in your life? Write it down in as much detail as possible.

_____

_____

_____

A.1. Who are your potential customers?

_____

_____

_____

A.2.a. What do you think they want in your service/product?

_____

_____

A.2.b. What kinds of things might they like about your service/product?

_____

A.2.c. Why would they NOT use your product or service?

_____

A.2.d. How could you address this resistance?

_____

A.3. Where do these folks live, worship, have fun, etc?

_____

_____

_____

B. If you want to create abundance within the structure of your current job, how will you make more money? (For instance, can you do this through a raise, or a promotion?)

_____

B.1. What will it take to create that?

_____

B.2. Do you need to get more education to be promoted? Is there a move you can make and do laterally that will create more wealth?

_____

_____

B.3. How do you feel about your current job? What are its benefits and costs in terms of quality of life?

_____

_____

B.3.a. Is your job sucking the life out of you? Can you transfer to another department or job, or can you work for another company doing something similar?

_____

_____

B.4. Is there a person at work who is safe to talk to about opportunities within your company? How can you help each other out?

_____

B.5. How can you make your supervisor see how indispensible and important you are for the work place?

_____

_____

C. What's the big picture? What specifically do you want out of life? How do you want your life to be different as a result of having done the work in this book?

_____

_____

C.1. What tasks will it take to get the big picture? Do you see specific steps that you must take?

_____

_____

C.2. What actions will you take to get that big picture?

_____

_____

C.3. What can you do today to start building the foundation for the big picture?

_____

_____

_____

C.4. What do you need to tell yourself to keep motivated?

_____

_____

_____

C.5. Who can help you along the way? How can you help them back?

_____

_____

D. Are you ready to start? What resistance do you have to starting tomorrow?

_____

E. How will you ensure that you have all types of wealth in your life? How will you take care of yourself physically, spiritually, emotionally and socially?

_____

_____

E. Would it help you to chart your progress visually? Here's a sample that might help organize these action steps in a real-world sequence:

Today's date	Bigger goal	Specific Action	Date started	Target date (when you want to have it completed)	Date completed

Now, pick a goal buddy or buddies with whom you plan to keep in contact after reading this book or completing this workshop. Keep in touch with them at least every other week. Each person can check in for about half an hour each meeting. Talk about how you're progressing with your goals. Help each other with your definitions of wealth and abundance as you go along; it might change in the process. That change is a sign of active minds and spirits, so it's good! It's helpful to say encouraging things to each other. Be realistic as well; try to find a balance between realism and optimism and encouragement to help them to keep their commitment strong. You can help them as best you can, but you don't want to work harder on their goals than they are working. Keep in mind that you each are responsible for your own success. Do not let yourselves get distracted. You can support each other very well if you both stay the course.

You're on your way – woo-hoo!

CREATING ABUNDANT WEALTH WORKBOOK

PRE-WORKSHOP / PRE-BOOK SURVEY

Name: _____   Age: _____   Gender: _____

Current Occupation: _____

Desired Occupation: _____

What do you hope this workshop or book can do for you?

_____

What are your goals for creating financial wealth?

_____

_____

What do you plan to do to reach your goals?

_____

_____

How do you know that you have been successful?

_____

_____

On a scale of 1 to 10, 10 being the most ready to achieve your goals, please rate how you feel right now? _____

Thank you for completing this. It will help both you and me in gauging how successful this process has been for you at the end.

Lisa S. Larsen, PsyD

CREATING ABUNDANT WEALTH WORKBOOK

POST-WORKSHOP / POST-BOOK SURVEY

Name: _____ Age: _____ Gender: _____

Current Occupation: _____

Desired Occupation: _____

Please rate the workshop on the following criteria (10 being the best, 1 being the worst):

Please answer for yourself how this course or book has been able to help in the following areas:	1	2	3	4	5	6	7	8	9	10
Able to meet any of your goals										
Satisfied with how the workshop was led										
Satisfied with the learning materials provided										
Likely to have a good mixture of all kinds of wealth in your life (physical health, spiritual, etc.)										
Less likely to work compulsively										
More informed about money and its management										
Able to define wealth for yourself										
Use your wealth wisely and considerately										
More informed about your own beliefs about money										
More informed about inner resistance to abundance										
Satisfied with realizing your hopes for this workshop / book										
Able to make a realistic, doable action plan										
More likely to get out and network										
More likely to save your money										
Less likely to spend money compulsively										
Glad that you took this course/read this book										

Lisa S. Larsen, PsyD

Tell me three things I could improve this workshop / book

_____

_____

Tell me three things that you did like about this workshop / book

_____

_____

What other feedback or suggestions do you have for the book or workshop?

_____

_____

On a scale of 1 to 10, 10 being the closest you can be meeting your goals, how close are you today? _____

If you read this book and did not take the workshop, I would still love to hear from you. Please feel free to email comments/suggestions to lisalarsen69@gmail.com. Your input is valuable to me and I'd love to know how I can improve this book as well.

Thank you!

_____

ABOUT THE AUTHOR

Lisa S. Larsen, PsyD is a licensed psychologist from the San Francisco Bay Area. After working in alcohol and drug programs and nonprofit settings, she was in private practice in the San Francisco Bay Area. Then she relocated to the Antelope Valley in 2009 and has been in private practice there since then. Her specialties are trauma recovery and addictions. In working with people who have compulsive behaviors, she has noticed a connection between feelings of emptiness and anxiety, and compulsive spending. Along the way, she has helped many people examine their thoughts and behaviors when it comes to money and this has helped them gain a better grasp of their lives in general, and their finances in specific. Her mission is to heal and empower people with consciousness about their beliefs, attitudes and behaviors.

If you live in the Antelope Valley, please call her regarding workshop opportunities to use this workbook live with other participants. You can visit her website for more information about her: www.yourtraumatherapist.com.

www.ingramcontent.com/pod-product-compliance
Lightning Source LLC
Chambersburg PA
CBHW081016040426
42444CB00014B/3236